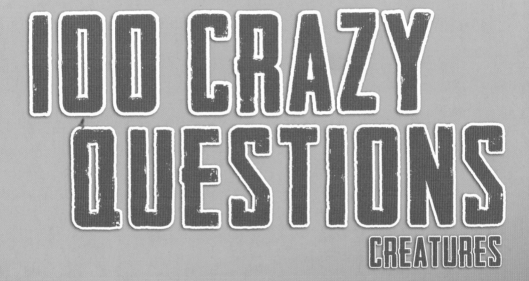

100 CRAZY QUESTIONS

CREATURES

BEN GROSSBLATT

becker&mayer! kids

CONTENTS

REPTILES

WHAT'S THE SILLIEST ANIMAL QUESTION YOU CAN THINK OF?

CAN A SHARK EAT A CAR?

DO NARWHALS SWORD FIGHT?

WHAT WOULD HAPPEN IF A GORILLA WENT TO THE GYM?

It's fun to get silly. In this book, we put together 100 of the silliest animal questions we could think up, then giggled a lot about those questions. And then we got serious and answered them with *real* science.

The answers—and the facts we learn as we get to those answers—may surprise you. Let's get real: the animal kingdom can be completely bizarre. Just about anything you can think of, some animal can do it. Which is more out-there, the questions or the answers? We don't know, but here's the point: it's about to get totally wild in here.

Furry, feathered, or finned. Flying, swimming, digging deep, or hanging from a tree. Animals are awesome, and their abilities and adaptations can sometimes seem unbelievable.

AMPHIBIANS

When you think of amphibians, think of the word *both*: amphibians need *both* water and land to complete their life cycle. For most amphibians, this means starting life as a larva (or tadpole if you're a frog or a toad) in the water. They swim around until they get big enough to try out life on land. They grow legs and sometimes lose their tails and become land dwellers. Amphibians have lungs, but they can also—wait for it—breathe (and absorb water) *through their skin*. Some make poison. Some are vibrant and bright. And some can really surprise you.

WHAAAT?!

Axolotls are found in the wild in only one place—the Xochimilco Lake complex near Mexico City. That's right: axolotls live in a secret lair!

WHAT MAKES AXOLOTLS LIKE SUPERBABIES?

WHAT DO WE KNOW?

First of all, what's an axolotl (AK-suh-la-tul)? These adorable little amphibians are a rare kind of salamander, known for their smiley, frilled faces. Axolotls hang on to their juvenile form for their whole lives. While other amphibians—and other creatures—start as youngsters and then grow up, changing along the way, axolotls keep their kid traits forever. Usually, they live in the water their whole lives, never transitioning to the land. They keep the dorsal fin that tadpoles are known for. And while they do develop lungs, they also keep their weird, feathery, completely outside-the-body gills. So that's the "baby" part of the axolotl story. Now, what's so super about them?

ANSWER: THEY CAN GROW, BABY, GROW!

This is where it gets good. Lots of animals can regenerate, or regrow, certain specific injured parts. But for an axolotl this is like a genuine superpower. It can totally regenerate almost any missing body part perfectly. Arms, legs, tails, jaws—they can regrow them all, with no scarring or anything!

CREATURE FEATURES

Axolotl
Ambystoma mexicanum
Length: Up to 12 inches (30 cm)
Weight: Up to 8 ounces (226 g)
Location: Mexico

WHAT IF YOU WIPED YOUR HANDS ON A POISON DART FROG?

WHAT DO WE KNOW?

Look, it's right there in the name: *poison* dart frog. Though not all poison dart frogs are actually poisonous, a number of them release toxins through their skin. These frogs are so named because indigenous hunters of Central and South America would rub the tips of their blow darts on the frogs' backs. This made blowgun attacks double deadly. If the darts didn't finish off the hunters' prey, the frog poison would. (The beautifully named golden poison frog has enough poison in its tiny body to kill 10 adult humans.) Scientists aren't sure how these frogs turn toxic, but some think it might be toxic stuff in the plants eaten by the insects the frogs eat.

ANSWER: DO *NOT* DO THIS.

If you did, you might be in big trouble. While not all poison dart frogs are poisonous, and not all of them are poisonous to touch, it's true that with some frogs, a touch is all it takes. The good news is that it's hard to do this on purpose. These frogs even come packaged in bright colors to warn you—and the frogs' natural predators—away. The bold patterns and their blues, reds, yellows, and greens are signs that the frogs are not nice to eat and are potentially deadly.

CREATURE FEATURES

Poison dart frog
More than 100 species in the family Dendrobatidae
Length: Up to about 1.5 inches (4 cm)
Weight: Less than 1 ounce (up to 20 g)
Location: Central and South America

BIRDS

Birds have wings, feathers, and light, hollow bones. And they all lay eggs. From ostriches—which, at 9 feet (2.7 m) tall, can tower above you—to hummingbirds so small you could practically stick one behind your ear like a pencil, birds come in an incredible variety of shapes, sizes, and special abilities. There are birds that can outrun the fastest human, birds that can fly upside down, and birds that hunt in almost total silence.

WHAAAT?!

They're not handy but footy: Bald eagles can swoop down to snatch fish out of the water with their strong talons.

ARE BALD EAGLES GOOD WITH THEIR HANDS?

WHAT DO WE KNOW?

Well, we know they definitely don't have hands. But bald eagles are famous for lots of things: their strength, their size, their overall majesty, and the way they appear on American quarters. But while you're remembering all that, don't forget their impressive construction abilities.

ANSWER: NO, BUT THE TRUTH IS, BALD EAGLES ARE ABOUT AS HANDY AS ANYTHING WITH NO ACTUAL HANDS CAN BE.

The nests they build, called aeries (AIR-eez), command the best views from tall trees. Bald eagles prefer building their nests as high as 138 feet (42 m) above the ground. The male and female of a bald eagle pair build the nest together. An aerie starts as a mound of sticks, then the eagles line the structure with softer stuff. They come back year after year to add to the nest for each new batch of eaglets. These cozy eagle homes, where the eaglets are fed and raised by both parents, can grow to be 6 feet (2 m) across.

CREATURE FEATURES

Bald eagle
Haliaeetus leucocephalus
Length: Up to 3.5 feet (1 m)
Wingspan: Up to 8 feet (2.4 m)
Weight: Up to 18 pounds (8.2 kg)
Location: Much of North America

IS THE SIX-PLUMED BIRD OF PARADISE GOING TO BE A STAR ONE DAY?

WHAT DO WE KNOW?

Birds of paradise are actually a whole family of bird species. They're known for their colorful, eye-catching plumage—and the males' wild courtship dances. And the six-plumed bird of paradise is no exception.

ANSWER: HE IS ALREADY A STAR.

The six-plumed bird of paradise is a total pro. Before his audience shows up, he actually cleans up the forest floor—he clears all the leaves away, polishes branches, moves twigs. When a female comes by for a look, it's showtime. The six-plumed bird of paradise spreads out a skirt of feathers and shakes his head, making his long, spindly plumes bob. He spreads a collar of shiny yellow, green, and blue feathers to dazzle her. He shimmies and prances. And at the end, there's nothing left to do but wait for the reviews. What does his audience of one think?

CREATURE FEATURES

Bird of paradise
About 40 species in the family Paradisaeidae
Length: 6 inches (15 cm)–3.5 feet (1 m), depending on the species
Weight: 2 ounces (57 g)–1 pound (0.5 kg), depending on the species
Location: New Guinea and northeastern Australia

There are 39 species of birds of paradise in the wild, and they're all amazing looking! Here are just a few.

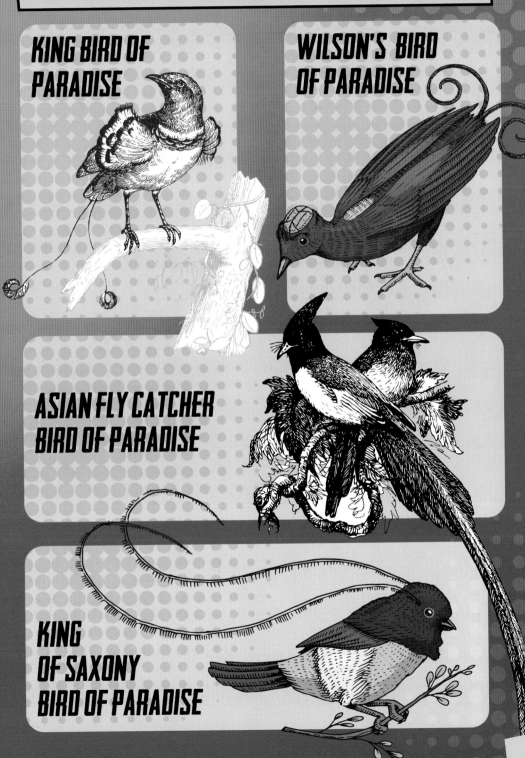

KING BIRD OF PARADISE

WILSON'S BIRD OF PARADISE

ASIAN FLY CATCHER BIRD OF PARADISE

KING OF SAXONY BIRD OF PARADISE

HOW WOULD AN EMPEROR PENGUIN DO IN A GAME OF HIDE-AND-SEEK?

WHAT DO WE KNOW?

Emperor penguins are the biggest species of penguins, tiptoeing up to nearly 4 feet (1.2 m) tall. Like most penguins, they're black and white, but these guys also have a tint of orange near their beaks. But what about their hiding skills?

ANSWER: IT ALL DEPENDS— WHERE ARE THE EMPERORS TRYING TO HIDE?

If they're in the waters of Antarctica, then, yes. In that case, they are definitely good at playing hide-and-seek. Like many animals that make their living in the sea, emperor penguins exhibit what is called countershading. That means their backs are dark (so they're hard to spot from above, when looking down into the darkness of the water), and their bellies are light (which makes them hard to see from below, when looking up toward the sun). This lets them hunt fish and squid effectively, and it helps them avoid being hunted by leopard seals and orcas.

But what if the emperor penguins are on the ice? Let's put it this way: there aren't a lot of places to hide on the Antarctic ice.

Emperor Penguin   **Macaroni Penguin**   **Galapagos Penguin**

CREATURE FEATURES

Emperor penguin
Aptenodytes forsteri
Length: Almost 4 feet (1.2 m)
Weight: Up to 88 pounds (40 kg)
Location: Antarctica

DO HUMMINGBIRDS COME FROM A DIFFERENT DIMENSION?

WHAT DO WE KNOW?

Hummingbirds do everything superfast. Here are some numbers to consider. A hummingbird's heart rate during flight can be as fast as 20 beats per second. (That's about six times your fastest possible heart rate.) Its wings can beat 80 times per second. And if it needs to get rain off of itself, it can shake its head 19 times per second. Relative to size, hummingbirds can fly faster than F15 Eagle fighter jets. During migration, some hummingbirds can fly for 20 hours straight, no refueling necessary. Hummingbirds can hover, fly backward, and even fly upside down. These are all out-of-this-world abilities. Are they truly from another plane of existence?

ANSWER: NO. THEY MIGHT NOT BE FROM ANOTHER DIMENSION, BUT THEY CAN DEFINITELY MOVE IN MORE DIMENSIONS.

Out of all four-limbed creatures, only hummingbirds have brains that can handle true multidirectional movement. The brains of all other four-limbed animals have a built-in preference for moving forward and backward—ahead, toward food, or backward, away from threats. It's like only hummingbirds really live in three dimensions.

CREATURE FEATURES

Hummingbird
More than 300 species in the family Trochilidae
Length: Up to 9 inches (23 cm)
Weight: Up to 1 ounce (28 g)
Location: North and South America

ARE KIWIS JUST PRETENDING TO BE BIRDS?

WHAT DO WE KNOW?

Think about what makes a bird a bird and take a look at the evidence. Typically, birds have wings, lay eggs in nests, and have hollow bones that are lightweight and suitable for flight.

Kiwis have solid bones, lay eggs in burrows, and have teeny tiny wings about an inch (2.5 cm) long. And their wings are tipped with little claws! They also have hairy feathers, skin that's thick and tough—very unbirdlike—and whiskers. And they have no tails. They grunt, hiss, and purr. And their nostrils are located all the way at the tips of their beaks, unlike every other bird on earth, whose nostrils are closer to their head. Another thing that sets them apart from most birds: they mark their territory with droppings. Also, just look at them!

ANSWER: IT'S CONTROVERSIAL TO SAY IT, BUT IT JUST MIGHT BE TRUE: KIWI BIRDS ARE, IN FACT, JUST PRETENDING.

All right, all right. Kiwis are actually birds of course, just really strange ones. They have feathers, and they lay eggs. That makes them birds in anybody's book.

CREATURE FEATURES

Kiwi
5 species in the genus *Apteryx*
Length: Up to 25 inches (64 cm)
Weight: Up to 11 pounds (5 kg)
Location: New Zealand

WHAAAT?!

These little birds have long lives. They can live to be up to 50 years old!

No tail!

Hairy feathers!

Teeny, tiny wings!

Legs made for running!

Nostrils far down their beak!

WHAT IS AN OSTRICH'S FAVORITE THING?

WHAT DO WE KNOW?

It's hard to know for sure—ostriches aren't known for talking a lot about themselves—but we could look at what they spend lots of their time on.

ANSWER: IT PROBABLY HAS SOMETHING TO DO WITH THEIR EGGS.

Ostriches seem to put a lot of energy into their eggs. That shouldn't be surprising. Ostrich eggs are pretty special. They're the biggest eggs in the world, measuring 6 inches (15 cm) long and weighing in at 3 pounds (1.4 kg). That's about the same size and weight as a cantaloupe. The dominant male of the herd makes the nest, a shallow depression in the ground, and the alpha female lays her eggs (as many as 10 of them) in the center. Then all the other females of the herd join in, laying their eggs in the same nest. The top male and female take turns sitting on and protecting the herd's huge collection of eggs until they hatch. Then the hatchlings are raised by their parents.

WHAAAT?!

Ostriches don't just have big eggs—ostrich eyes are the biggest of any land animal.

Ostrich   Goose   Chicken

CREATURE FEATURES

Ostrich
Struthio camelus
Height: Up to 9 feet (2.7 m)
Weight: About 280 pounds (127 kg)
Location: Central and southern Africa

WHAT IF OWLS CARRIED THEIR KEYS IN THEIR POCKETS?

WHAT DO WE KNOW?

Birds like hawks and falcons depend on speed, but owls depend on silence for their hunting success. Owls hunt at night, hiding in the darkness, and they're designed to be quiet hunters. Their feathers are almost furry, which lets them move over each other noiselessly. Tiny comblike structures on owls' wing feathers—called fimbriae (FIM-bree-ee)—break up the wind as the owls fly, and the feathers are shaggy, too—there's almost no rustling sound to tell prey animals that something's coming for them. An owl doesn't need to flap its big, broad wings very often to stay in the air. And they can glide more slowly than other birds. That, too, means less noise. It's like everything about owls is optimized for stealthy hunting.

ANSWER: JINGLING KEYS WOULD MEAN OWLS COULD NO LONGER RELY ON STEALTH, AND WHAT'S AN OWL WITHOUT STEALTH?

If owls carried their keys in their pockets, it would totally cramp their style. A slow, noisy hunter would come up empty every time. (Also, owls don't have pockets.)

CREATURE FEATURES

Owl
About 200 species in the order Strigiformes
Height: 5–28 inches (13–71 cm), depending on the species
Weight: 1.5 ounces (43 g)–9 pounds (4 kg), depending on the species
Location: Worldwide

CAN A *PARROT* RECITE THE *ALPHABET* *BACKWARD?*

WHAT DO WE KNOW?

These birds have shown that they're very intelligent. Take Alex, an African gray parrot who became famous for his brainy feats. He knew more than 100 words, and he knew his numbers, too. In fact, Alex amazed everyone by being able to count and even add. Was Alex just, you know, parroting people? Mimicking their speech? No, Alex really knew the names for all kinds of objects and concepts, and he combined them in new ways. The first time he saw a birthday cake, he didn't know what it was. After he tried some, he declared it "yummy bread." Maybe Alex was unique, an Einstein among parrots? Well, the researcher who would go on to spend so much time teaching and studying him asked the guy at the local pet store to grab any old gray parrot. It turned out to be Alex. So if any old parrot could do all that stuff . . .

ANSWER: PROBABLY. IT'S A SAFE BET THAT NO PARROT HAS EVER DONE THIS, BUT THERE'S NO REASON ONE COULDN'T.

WHAAAT?!

A parakeet is a type of small parrot. One parakeet named Puck knew more than 1,700 words.

CREATURE FEATURES

Parrot
More than 350 species in the order Psittaciformes
Height: Up to 40 inches (102 cm)
Weight: About 3.5 pounds (1.6 kg)
Location: Mostly in the Southern Hemisphere

CAN A TOUCAN KNOCK YOU OUT WITH ITS BIG BEAK?

WHAT DO WE KNOW?

In some toucan species, the big wedge-shaped beak can be almost as long as the rest of the bird's body.

ANSWER: NO. A TOUCAN'S BEAK IS FAR TOO LIGHT TO HARM YOU.

It has to be—if toucan bills were as heavy as they look, toucans could never balance way out on the ends of small branches. So what does the toucan use its beak for, if not whacking prey, predators, and rivals?

Scientists now believe that a toucan uses its beak to keep cool in its tropical climate. Just like an elephant's ears help it radiate heat, toucans use their beaks to regulate their body temperature. And with those brilliant greens, yellows, oranges, and blues, toucan beaks are beautiful and eye catching. So while a toucan's beak can't knock you out, it's still a real knockout. Best. Toucan pun. Ever. (Second-best toucan pun: Why do toucans like to play doubles tennis? Because tou-can play at that game.)

White-throated toucan

CREATURE FEATURES

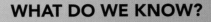 Toucan

More than 40 species in the family Ramphastidae
Height: 12 inches (30 cm)–24 inches (61 cm), depending on the species
Weight: 3.5 ounces (99 g)–2 pounds (0.9 kg), depending on the species
Location: Central and South America

Angler fish

Stingray

Longhorn cowfish

Siamese fighting fish

Flowerhorn cichlid

Radiata lionfish

Grouper

Giant frogfish

Whale shark

FISH

You might think you know all you need to know about fish. But these guys do much more than swim around. There are around 30,000 species of fish—and they include everything from your pet goldfish to huge rays and even sharks. Some fish are predators with jaws big enough to chomp their prey in half. Some are poisonous creatures that just want to be left alone. Some are sleek and beautiful. Some are fearsome and even a little bit ugly. (Sorry, but it's true.) Some are brilliantly colorful, and some are masters of camouflage. If it can be done, fish can do it.

CAN A HAMMERHEAD SHARK SEE AROUND CORNERS?

WHAT DO WE KNOW?

Trick question! There are no corners in the ocean! But what if there were? Would a hammerhead shark's big, wide face let it see around them? Those far-apart eyes supply the shark with incredible, panoramic vision. A slight turn of its head, and it can see all the way behind it. And its head is extremely sensitive, too—it's covered by more special electricity receptors than other sharks have. So it can detect prey animals even when they hide in the sand. (Nice try, prey.) But that's not all. A hammerhead's wide-set nostrils help it home in on scent signals in the water, and it uses its flat head to pin stingrays against the ocean floor. The hammer-shaped head might even help the shark make its famous whip-quick turns.

ANSWER: NO. BUT WHILE IT DOESN'T ALLOW FOR SEEING AROUND CORNERS, A HAMMERHEAD'S WEIRD-SHAPED HEAD IS STILL THE SOURCE OF ITS AMAZING HUNTING POWERS.

CREATURE FEATURES

Hammerhead shark
9 species in the family Sphyrnidae
Length: 13–20 feet (4–6 m), depending on the species
Weight: 500–1,000 pounds (227–454 kg), depending on the species
Locations: Oceans around the world

CAN A GREAT WHITE SHARK EAT A CAR?

WHAT DO WE KNOW?

First off, would a shark want to do this? No, it wouldn't want to eat a car—there's no meat in it. But what if you were the meat inside the car? The good news: Great whites attack plenty of people (as many as half of all shark attacks on humans are great white attacks) but not usually on purpose. Scientists think great whites attack humans when they mistake them for seals or sea lions. The bad news: Sharks have certainly been known to attack boats and other large objects. Maybe they're drawn to them because of the electrical fields generated by certain metals corroding in seawater. Or maybe they're drawn to the electrical field generated by boat motors.

So what if a shark got it in its head to go after your car? Great whites are famous for their enormous jaws and nightmarish teeth, but it's their bite strength that matters here. By one measure of bite force, which compares an animal's bite strength to its size, Nile crocodiles have jaws that are more than twice as strong.

ANSWER: IF A GREAT WHITE DID CHOMP ON A CAR, IT WOULD PROBABLY PUNCTURE THE DOOR, LOSE A BUNCH OF TEETH, AND GIVE UP.

CREATURE FEATURES

Great white shark
Carcharodon carcharias
Length: Up to 20 feet (6 m)
Weight: Up to 4,500 pounds (2,042 kg)

WHAAAT?!

A great white shark might replace 20,000 teeth in its lifetime.

IS A RED LIONFISH COMING SOON TO AN OCEAN NEAR YOU?

WHAT DO WE KNOW?

If there's one thing lionfish are known for—beyond their beautiful fanlike fins, the venomous spines along their backs, their prey-herding behavior, and their impressive appetites—it's their "march" across the globe. The native range of the lionfish is the warm waters of the Indo-Pacific region, from Australia to the east coast of Africa. But somehow (spoiler: it was probably American pet owners releasing them when they didn't want them in their aquariums anymore, and Hurricane Andrew might have played a role in lionfish escaping from pet stores), lionfish have made their way to the Caribbean and the East Coast of the United States. And in that new territory, lionfish have no natural predators. They reproduce throughout the year, so they keep multiplying and spreading. Some scientists are worried that lionfish will even damage reef ecosystems by eating the fish that eat seaweed, which might result in seaweed wrecking the reefs.

Pacific Ocean

ANSWER: YES, IF THE OCEAN NEAR YOU HAS WARM WATER.

CREATURE FEATURES

Red lionfish
Pterois volitans
Length: Up to 15 inches (38 cm)
Weight: Up to 2.6 pounds (1.2 kg)
Location: Native to the Western Pacific Ocean

WHAAAT?!

A lionfish can release 2,000,000 eggs a year.

 Bermuda

Pacific Ocean

Atlantic Ocean

Indian Ocean

Pterois volitans

Pterois miles

Nonnative Pterois volitans and Pterois miles

COULD A MANTA RAY FLY THROUGH THE AIR?

WHAT DO WE KNOW?

In the water, a manta ray glides powerfully and serenely, like a cross between a mermaid and an eagle. Still, mobulas (cousins of manta rays) are known to leap from the water and fly. Kind of. When they launch themselves into the air, they manage a few feeble flaps before falling back into the ocean.

ANSWER: SADLY, NO.

It takes much more force to beat your wings against the air and stay aloft than it does to push yourself through the water. Let's be honest, though: even if rays like the mobulas are not actually flying, seeing them leap is an amazing sight. One after the other, hundreds of mobulas, looking like sleek, black kites, pop from the waves and then drop back down, over and over, like skipping stones.

CREATURE FEATURES

Manta ray
2 species in the genus *Manta*
Width: Up to 23 feet (7 m)
Weight: Up to 5,300 pounds (2,400 kg)
Location: Warm and temperate waters around the world

KNOW YOUR RAYS

There are more than 500 species of rays swimming the world's oceans. Here are just a few:

MOBULA RAY

Mobula rays swim in schools of more than 100 rays.

GUITAR FISH

Instrument-shaped rays live on the bottom of the sea and gobble up shellfish and shrimp.

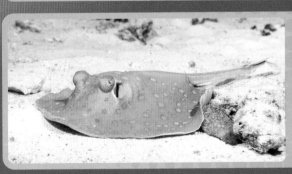

STINGRAY

Stingray tails have venomous barbs at the end.

SAWFISH

These rays have up to 23 teeth lining their sawlike snouts.

CAN YOU PLAY VOLLEYBALL WITH A PUFFER FISH?

WHAT DO WE KNOW?

Wait, do you mean the puffer fish is your volleyball teammate? No! They don't have any arms, silly. If you mean "play with it" as in using it for a volleyball, that might be a different story. Setting aside the fact that it's a fish and needs to be in the water, many puffer fish are covered in spines. That would make the fish-volleyball unpleasant for the players and the fish. Add to that the deadly tetrodotoxin poison found in most puffer fish and it's definitely game over. Though this toxin is mostly internal—that means you definitely don't want to eat one—this stuff is more than a thousand times more deadly than cyanide, and there might be enough of it in one puffer fish to kill 30 people. It could take out the players on both volleyball teams, the coaches, and a bunch of spectators!

ANSWER: NO! DON'T DO IT! IT'S SURE TO END VERY BADLY FOR THE PLAYERS AND THE POOR PUFFER FISH.

WHAAAT?!

Puffer fish—also called blowfish—usually fill themselves up with water, not air. Just another reason why they'd make really bad volleyballs.

CREATURE FEATURES

Puffer fish
190 species in the family
Tetraodontide
Length: Up to 2 feet
(0.6 m)
Weight: Varies
Location: Oceans around
the world

INVERTEBRATES

Invertebrates are everywhere. No, no, you don't understand. They are everywhere. There might even be one on you right now! (Made you look.) Something like 97 percent of *all animal species on the planet* are invertebrates. You see, invertebrates aren't a single kind of organism. An invertebrate is an animal without a backbone or skeleton. That makes insects invertebrates. And arachnids. And cephalopods, like octopuses and squids. And jellyfish. And worms. And snails. And many, many other groups of animals.

IS AN ATLAS MOTH A PICKY EATER?

WHAT DO WE KNOW?

In caterpillar form, atlas moths are healthy eaters, dining on the leaves of fruit trees. Adults will refuse to eat everything you put in front of them. Although, to be honest, that's not actually because they're picky. It's because they don't have working mouths, so they couldn't eat anything even if they wanted to.

ANSWER: YES. ATLAS MOTHS ARE AMONG THE PICKIEST EATERS ON THE PLANET—OR THE HUNGRIEST, BECAUSE OF THE NO-MOUTH THING.

No mouth? How does that work? How can the atlas moth survive without eating? Simple: it doesn't. About two weeks after emerging from its cocoon, an atlas moth mates, lays eggs (you know, if it's female), and then dies.

One way they survive for those two weeks is thanks to a neat kind of camouflage. Take a look at the pattern on the corners of an atlas moth's upper wings. If you squint, it looks like a cobra's head in profile. And it might be that predators are squinting at them, too, and deciding not to eat the atlas moth. Who wants to tangle with a cobra?

WHAAAT?!

The atlas moth is one of the biggest moths in the world.

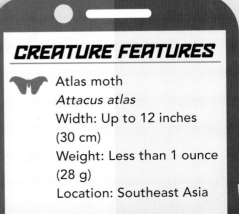

CREATURE FEATURES

Atlas moth
Attacus atlas
Width: Up to 12 inches (30 cm)
Weight: Less than 1 ounce (28 g)
Location: Southeast Asia

HOW DOES A BOMBARDIER BEETLE LEVEL UP?

WHAT DO WE KNOW?

Picture it: the bombardier beetle, an unassuming little bug, is minding its own business, when a potential predator starts making trouble. Prey in this situation has a few options: it can run, hide, or fight back.

ANSWER: THE BOMBARDIER BEETLE DEFINITELY CHOOSES OPTION NUMBER 3—IT LEVELS UP AND TURNS INTO A WALKING EXPLOSION FACTORY.

Inside its abdomen, special chambers are filled with special chemicals, and when a special valve opens between the chambers, the chemicals mix and a *very* special chemical reaction takes place. The resulting liquid is steaming hot (literally), and it shoots out of the beetle's butt from a nozzle the beetle can aim with surprising accuracy.

Why doesn't this trick hurt the beetle? The secret is in the way the bombardier's biological machinery pulses. Instead of firing out in a steady stream, the nasty liquid spits out in hundreds of little pulses every second. This on-off-on system gives the beetle's insides a chance to cool just enough to avoid being damaged.

CREATURE FEATURES

Bombardier beetle
Subfamily Brachininae
Length: Less than 1 inch (2.5 cm)
Weight: Less than 1 ounce (28 g)
Location: All continents except Antarctica

WALKING EXPLOSION FACTORY

These little beetles pack a steaming hot surprise! Their explosive spray protects them from predators.

CAN YOU USE A DEATHSTALKER SCORPION AS A FLASHLIGHT?

WHAT DO WE KNOW?

Deathstalkers and other scorpions do glow in the right conditions. Which, when you think about it, is eerie and cool. Special molecules in a layer of the scorpion's exoskeleton absorb ultraviolet (UV) light and give it back as a blue-green glow. People even use this in order to find scorpions at night: they shine a UV light, and any scorpions under the beam glow. (All of this raises another question: Why does anybody *want* to find scorpions in the dark?) Scientists aren't sure why scorpions work this way. One intriguing theory is that it helps scorpions hide effectively from predators, like some rodents and birds of prey. The scorpions' bodies absorb UV light from the moon and turn it into a glow that tells them they're in a place where predators can spot them, too.

ANSWER: NO, BUT THEY DO LOOK REALLY COOL UNDER UV LIGHT.

And PS: Don't even pick up any scorpions, ever. They pack a nasty sting.

CREATURE FEATURES

Deathstalker scorpion
Leiurus quinquestriatus
Length: About 4 inches (10 cm)
Weight: 0.09 ounces (28 g)
Location: Northeastern Africa and the Middle East

HOW ARE DRAGONFLIES LIKE LIONS?

WHAT DO WE KNOW?

Dragonflies are incredibly fast. Not just their flying speed but also their *seeing* speed. They can process 200 images per second. (Humans can process about 60. Imagine watching the pages of a flipbook as they riffle past.) Their eyes are huge—most of a dragonfly's brain is devoted to vision—and they can see everything except the spot right behind them. And a dragonfly's reaction time is phenomenally fast.

When you compare dragonflies' rates of hunting success, well, lions look pretty shabby. (And they can't even hover!) Researchers found that dragonflies came back with prey in about 95 percent of attempts, which is far, far better than lions or other big cats.

ANSWER: MAYBE THE QUESTION SHOULD BE "HOW ARE DRAGONFLIES BETTER THAN LIONS?"

If you could shrink a lion down to dragonfly size, the "king of the jungle" would easily be shown up by these four-winged predators. (Read about lions on page 93 of this book.) Lions are famous for their ferocity and their hunting skills, but dragonflies would leave lions in the dust.

CREATURE FEATURES

Dragonfly
About 3,000 species in the suborder *Anisoptera*
Length: Up to 5 inches (12.7 cm)
Weight: Less than 1 ounce (or up to about 28 g)
Location: Everywhere but Antarctica

WHAAAT?!

A dragonfly's eye is made of about 28,000 facets.

41

DO MONARCH BUTTERFLIES SPEAK SPANISH?

WHAT DO WE KNOW?

Every year, monarchs fly to Mexico from as far away as Canada, and they never get lost. But check this out: they never even stop to ask for directions, so being able to speak Spanish might not be that important for the whole migration.

Apart from the sheer amazingness of an annual migration that covers thousands of miles and includes as many as a billion butterflies, the butterflies return to the same spots their ancestors visited, but no butterflies make the trip more than once. Let that sink in. Somehow, these insects know how to navigate these incredible distances, to go somewhere they've never been before.

In early spring, monarchs leave Mexico, heading north. One bunch lays eggs in Southern California. The eggs hatch, and about two weeks later the caterpillars make chrysalises and prepare to transform into butterflies. After another two weeks, they emerge. They head north. Their offspring make it little farther north. And the offspring of the offspring make it a little farther north. After three or four generations, the butterflies will have arrived at their northern homes in Canada and the United States. And the offspring of those butterflies will travel all the way to Mexico in August, and the whole cycle starts again.

ANSWER: NO, THEY DON'T SPEAK SPANISH. (WELL, THEY DON'T SPEAK.) BUT THEY DO SOMEHOW COMMUNICATE INFORMATION ACROSS GENERATIONS.

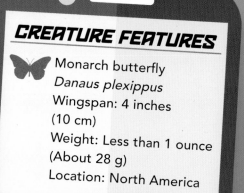

CREATURE FEATURES

Monarch butterfly
Danaus plexippus
Wingspan: 4 inches (10 cm)
Weight: Less than 1 ounce (About 28 g)
Location: North America

IS A NAUTILUS INTO HOME IMPROVEMENT?

WHAT DO WE KNOW?

First things first: a nautilus is a cephalopod, which puts it in the same class as octopuses and squids. Like those other creatures, a nautilus has tentacles (more than 90 of them!), but unlike them, a nautilus lives inside a beautiful spiral shell made of a series of separate compartments, or chambers. Sometimes people call nautiluses "living fossils," because they haven't changed much in hundreds of millions of years. But maybe they should call them living *submarines* because they rise and descend in the water thanks to inner chambers that can fill with gas (for being lighter and going up) or water (for being heavier and going down). When it starts its life, a nautilus lives in a shell of four chambers, and it keeps adding "rooms," until it ends up with around 30.

ANSWER: YES—INTO IT? A NAUTILUS IS A TOTAL HOME IMPROVEMENT FANATIC!

CREATURE FEATURES

Chambered nautilus
Nautilus pompilius
Length: Up to 8 inches (20 cm)
Weight: Less than 2 pounds (0.9 kg)
Location: Southeast Asia and Australia

WHAT IF
YOU PUT AN OCTOPUS IN A JAR?

WHAT DO WE KNOW?

More than 300 species of octopuses swim the oceans. They have speed, strength, and camouflage to outsmart predators and outdo prey. Their eight arms are covered in suction cups that allow them a tight grip. And they have no bones, which allows them to squeeze into and through tiny spaces. On top of that, scientists have long considered them to be the smartest invertebrate animals. Do you think an octopus could escape a lidded jar?

ANSWER: IT WOULD UNSCREW THE LID, OPEN THE TOP, AND ESCAPE EASILY, OF COURSE!

In fact, in 2010, scientists verified this feat. They submerged a jar in an aquarium and let the octopus crawl inside. They then closed the lid, and watched and waited.

Using its supersmarts, the octopus made quick work of figuring out the screw-top jar. It gripped the underside of the lid with its strong suction cups and turned with its arms. In just a few seconds, the octopus was out and about.

Octopuses can also open a jar from the outside—especially if there's a tasty treat inside.

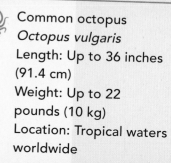

CREATURE FEATURES

Common octopus
Octopus vulgaris
Length: Up to 36 inches (91.4 cm)
Weight: Up to 22 pounds (10 kg)
Location: Tropical waters worldwide

WOULD A PORTUGUESE MAN-OF-WAR GET LOST IN THE MALL?

WHAT DO WE KNOW?

Surprise number 1: a Portuguese man-of-war isn't a jellyfish. Surprise number 2: a Portuguese man-of-war isn't an . . . anything. It's actually a colony of four separate organisms all living together as one superorganism. The top part is one organism called a pneumatophore (that's the name for the big inflatable bag that sits above the water and lends the Portuguese man-of-war its name—it reminded some people of the sail of a big ship called a man-of-war). The venomous tentacles are another organism, and the digestive and reproductive parts are the other two.

ANSWER: PROBABLY.

Portuguese man-of-wars have a terrible sense of direction. At least, they have no reason to know where they're going, because they have no way of moving on their own.

They just kick back and drift along in ocean currents, or let the breeze push their pneumatophores. They can also deflate their pneumatophores to sink.

Portuguese man-of-war
tentacles:
up to 165 feet (50 m)

Human
height:
6 feet
(1.8 m)

A Portuguese
man-of-war's
tentacles can be
more than 150
feet long!

CREATURE FEATURES

Portuguese man-of-war
Physalia physalis
Length: (the pneumato-
phore "sail") 12 inches
(30 cm)
Weight: Unknown
Location: Tropical and
subtropical waters around
the world

IF YOU WERE AN INCH HIGH, COULD YOU RIDE A SEAHORSE?

WHAT DO WE KNOW?

Seahorses aren't actually tiny, underwater horses, of course. There are many different species of seahorses ranging in size from 0.5 inches to 14 inches (1.3 cm to 36 cm). Seahorses move forward by quickly rippling a fin on their backs, and they're not very good swimmers. They get around better by grabbing seaweed with their tails and floating along with it. Seahorses might not be great at swimming, but they're excellent at camouflage. They can change color to hide from predators and sneak up on prey.

ANSWER: NO, YOU WOULDN'T BE ABLE TO RIDE A SEAHORSE. OR, WELL, YOU COULD TRY SITTING ON ONE—ALTHOUGH EVEN IF YOU WERE JUST AN INCH HIGH, YOU'D STILL BE TOO BIG FOR SOME SEAHORSES—BUT THE SEAHORSE WOULDN'T GET VERY FAR.

Carrying a rider would definitely interfere with their back fins, too.

WHAAAT?!

Male seahorses carry seahorse eggs in a pouch. When they're fully formed, the babies—hundreds of them in some species—race out of the pouch. They need to hide from predators right away.

CREATURE FEATURES

Seahorse
47 species in the genus *Hippocampus*
Length: Half an inch (1.3 cm) to more than 14 inches (36 cm)
Weight: Up to 1 pound (0.5 kg), depending on the species
Location: Tropical and temperate coastal waters

ARE STARFISH ACTUALLY ZOMBIES?

WHAT DO WE KNOW?

Instead of brains, starfish have nervous systems that are spread throughout their bodies. Instead of blood, they transport nutrients through their bodies using seawater, which sounds pretty efficient. If a starfish loses an arm, it can grow a new one. Scientists believe that some starfish can even grow a whole new body from a separated arm! And they have an eye at the end of each arm, too. So what about the eating habits of starfish? It starts when they pry open the shells of their prey. Then it gets really gross. Their stomachs emerge from their mouths, which are on the undersides of their body, surround the prey, and then digest it . . . outside the starfish's body. Then the starfish—gulp!—pulls its stomach back inside.

ANSWER: LET'S RUN DOWN THE ZOMBIE CHECKLIST. NO BRAINS? CHECK. NO BLOOD? CHECK. THE ABILITY TO CHEAT DEATH? CHECK. (STARFISH CAN REGENERATE, OR REGROW, BODY PARTS.) DISGUSTING EATING HABITS? CHECK. WELL, IT LOOKS LIKE STARFISH ARE INDEED ZOMBIES.

But really, they're echinoderms, which are creatures related to sand dollars, sea urchins, and sea cucumbers.

CREATURE FEATURES

Starfish (scientists prefer the term *sea star*)
About 2,000 species in the class Asteroidea
Width: Up to 3 feet (0.9 m)
Weight: Up to 13 pounds (5.9 kg)
Location: All over the world

WHAAAT?!

Most starfish species have 5 arms, but some have as many as 40!

WHAT'S LIFE LIKE IN TERMITE CITY?

WHAT DO WE KNOW?

In a termite colony—which can be home to millions of individuals—termites take on various jobs to help get things done and keep life running smoothly. There's even a kind of mayor, also known as the queen. (She lays the eggs—hundreds of millions of them over her lifetime.) Some termites farm fungus, to which they feed chewed-up wood and other plant matter that they can't digest on their own. The fungus breaks it down, the termites eat it, and then bacteria in the termites' bodies finish digesting it. The termite construction industry is booming especially in termite species in Africa. By hauling pieces of dirt, workers slowly build giant skyscrapers. Some species of termites labor for years on these monumental structures, which can rise more than 30 feet (9 m) above the African plain. Scientists are still studying these mounds and why termites make them. One recent theory is that the mounds are a way to keep good air flowing in and bad air flowing out for the termite colony.

ANSWER: IT SEEMS LIKE IT'S REALLY JUST A TINY INSECT VERSION OF LIFE IN A REGULAR PEOPLE-CITY.

WHAAAT?!

Some termites are soldiers: they have body parts that act as weapons in wars against invaders. Some termites fire noxious stuff from nozzles, and some leak sticky gel from special "backpacks."

CREATURE FEATURES

Termite

More than 2,500 species in the infraorder Isoptera

Length: About one-quarter of an inch (0.6 cm), but queens can be about 4 inches (10 cm) long

Weight: Less than 1 ounce (28 g)

Location: Tropical, subtropical, and temperate regions around the world

MAMMALS

What makes a mammal a mammal? All mammals have hair. Even elephants and whales. (And even your bald uncle Mike.) And all mammals—with the exceptions of those oddballs platypuses and echidnas—give birth to live young. In other words, no eggs for (almost all) mammals. And all mammal mothers make milk to feed their babies. Those are the defining features of mammals, but after that, all bets are off. Mammals can do just about anything: fly, glide, swim, run, dig, climb, build, invent, sing, play, and capture our hearts (awww). And just to be obvious about it, you're a mammal, too. And so is everyone in your family and your school. Note: This doesn't include the classroom turtle.

WOULD AN AARDVARK WANT TO RAID YOUR FRIDGE?

WHAT DO WE KNOW?

When it comes to termites and ants, aardvarks are on a mission. They are like termite-and-ant-locating and -eating machines. Aardvarks have strong claws and powerful digging feet to scrabble their way to the bugs even through tough termite mounds. And they've got long, sticky tongues to slurp the bugs up when they reach them. Thick skin protects the aardvark from bug bites. (Their big, rabbitlike ears are great for picking up the sounds of approaching predators.)

ANSWER: THIS PROBABLY WON'T HAPPEN, UNLESS YOU'RE KEEPING TERMITES AND ANTS IN THERE.

You're not keeping termites and ants in your fridge, are you? If you are, you should probably just open your fridge when the aardvarks come around and save them all that trouble. You might end up sparing your fridge, too.

CREATURE FEATURES

Aardvark
Orycteropus afer
Length: Up to 6.5 feet (2 m)
Weight: Up to 180 pounds (82 kg)
Location: Much of Africa

WHAAAT?!

When madly digging, an aardvark can close up its nostrils to keep dirt out of its nose.

ARE ALPACAS REALLY JUST LONG-NECKED DOGS?

WHAT DO WE KNOW?

Alpacas are cute, and they like hanging out with people. They have big canine teeth (!) and fuzzy coats. They're all domesticated, and they can easily be trained to do things like sit and get in and out of vehicles. (Does that remind you of any animals you know? Animals that might be living in your house with you right now?) They can even be brought inside and housebroken—yes, you can train them on where to go outside to do their business. I think they even tilt their heads in a doglike way! Fine, alpacas aren't actually dogs. Still . . . we're not quite ready to let this idea go.

ANSWER: NO. EVEN THOUGH IT SEEMS LIKE ALPACAS ARE ACTUALLY DOGS WITH REALLY LONG NECKS AND CAMEL FACES, THEY'RE NOT DOGS.

They're closely related to llamas. But they do make great companions—for people and dogs!

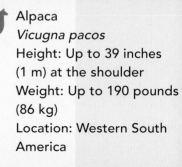

CREATURE FEATURES

Alpaca
Vicugna pacos
Height: Up to 39 inches (1 m) at the shoulder
Weight: Up to 190 pounds (86 kg)
Location: Western South America

WOULD AN ARCTIC FOX TAKE A TROPICAL VACATION?

WHAT DO WE KNOW?

Arctic foxes live in the frigid, snowy north. Which makes sense, when you consider all the ways Arctic foxes are suited to life in the cold. For starters, their ears, snouts, and legs are short, which means they lose less heat. If you live in a world where the temperatures get down to almost −60°F (−51°C), you need all the heat-holding help you can get. The bottoms of their feet are furry for warmth and traction on slippery terrain. And their famous bushy tails can double as blankets. Arctic foxes even have special coloring for the winter. Arctic foxes are the only canids—the group that also includes dogs and wolves—whose color changes like this. In the summer, Arctic foxes are brown or gray. But in the winter, their thick coats go white, so they can blend into their snowy surroundings.

ANSWER: PROBABLY NOT. IF AN ARCTIC FOX TOOK A VACATION TO SOMEPLACE WARM AND STEAMY, IT WOULD PROBABLY HAVE A LOUSY TIME.

CREATURE FEATURES

Arctic fox
Vulpes lagopus
Length: Up to 40 inches (1 m)
Weight: Up to 17 pounds (7.7 kg)
Location: The Arctic region around the world

WHAAAT?!

When prey is scarce, Arctic foxes survive on scraps left behind by polar bears and wolves.

CREATURE FEATURES

 Armadillo
20 species in the order Cingulata
Length: 6 inches (15 cm)–5 feet (1.5 m)
Weight: Up to 70 pounds (32 kg)
Location: South America, Central America, and parts of the southern United States

COULD AN ARMADILLO ROLL ITSELF DOWN A BOWLING ALLEY AND GET A STRIKE?

WHAT DO WE KNOW?

Out of 20 species of armadillos, only one—the three-banded armadillo—can actually roll up into a ball. They do this for protection. Those tough, leathery plates on an armadillo's back protect it from predators, such as birds of prey, wild cats, and even dogs. And when a three-banded armadillo tucks its head down, the little plate on top completes the shell, and the armadillo is completely shielded. When they roll up, they sometimes trap a predator's paw inside! Armadillos are excellent diggers, smellers, and hearers.

ANSWER: NO. UNFORTUNATELY FOR US, WHEN AN ARMADILLO ROLLS UP, IT'S REALLY JUST FORMING A STATIONARY BALL.

They can't actually roll, down a lane in a bowling alley or anywhere else.

WHAAAT?!

Pink fairy armadillos (which are *real*) are about 6 inches (15 cm) long. They look like they're wearing grubby pink capes.

WHAT WOULD HAPPEN IF A BAT WORE EARMUFFS?

WHAT DO WE KNOW?

So-called macrobats—bigger bats like fruitbats and flying foxes—don't usually rely on echolocation to find prey and navigate their environment. (Quick time-out! Echolocation means using sound to form a mental picture of the objects and surfaces around you. When you echolocate you make noises and use the echoes that come back to you to "see," even in total darkness.) Microbats—and some of them are really, really micro—often *do* depend on echolocation. Bats that eat small and quick-moving bugs need specialized parts for their click-and-listen hunting style. It's not just having ears that are sensitive to the superhigh-frequency sounds. It's also having faces that can help focus the sounds. (The peculiar sound-focusing structures on some bats' faces are known as nose leaves!) Did you know that close to a quarter of all mammal species are kinds of bats?

ANSWER: IT DEPENDS ON THE BAT.

If you outfitted a microbat with teeny tiny earmuffs, it would probably wreck the bat's ability to hunt and fly in the dark. Macrobats, the bigger ones that don't use echolocation, would just look cute.

WHAAAT?!

Mexican free-tailed bats send out special signals that confuse their bat rivals right when they're about to snap up a moth.

Bats send out sound waves through their mouths, which then bounce off of an object—like a yummy moth. Then the sound waves bounce back to the bat.

CREATURE FEATURES

Bat
About 1,300 species in the order Chiroptera
Wingspan: 0.5 feet (15 cm)–6 feet (1.8 m)
Weight: Less than 1 ounce (28 g)–2 pounds (0.9 kg)
Location: Worldwide, except for polar regions

Bat sonar

Returning sonar waves

ARE BEAVERS AFRAID OF THE DENTIST?

WHAT DO WE KNOW?

Beavers need superstrong teeth. Without them, they could never eat the tough plants they rely on or chew through all those branches and trees to make their lodges or giant dams. Beavers are built for chewing *and* for swimming. They've got webbed back feet, big lungs, waterproof coats, valves in their noses and ears to keep water out, and special goggle-like membranes over their eyes. They put it all to work constructing their homes and the dams that turn large areas into ponds.

ANSWER: NO. ONE LOOK AT A BEAVER'S BIG ORANGE TEETH, AND YOU MIGHT THINK, "THEY MIGHT NOT BE AFRAID OF THE DENTIST, BUT THEY'RE DEFINITELY OVERDUE FOR A TEETH CLEANING." IF YOU COULD LOOK CLOSER—MUCH, MUCH CLOSER, LIKE MICROSCOPE CLOSE—YOU'D THINK DIFFERENTLY.

That's because the enamel of beaver teeth has something special in it: iron. That's what makes their teeth that color. The iron also makes their teeth superstrong.

WHAAAT?!

The world's biggest beaver dam—first spotted in a satellite photo—was more than half a mile (0.8 km) long!

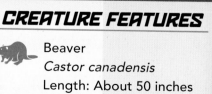

CREATURE FEATURES

Beaver
Castor canadensis
Length: About 50 inches (1.3 m)
Weight: 60 pounds (27 kg)
Location: North America

CAN A BISON FLIP YOUR CAR?

WHAT DO WE KNOW?

Bison are big. Or is it bisons are big? Either way, these are big animals. In fact, they're the heaviest land animals in North America. They can tip the scales at more than a ton (907 kg). Even with all that bulk, they're surprisingly fast, capable of reaching speeds of 35 miles (56 km) per hour. And they can get a bit grumpy, too. During mating season, males charge and crash into each other.

ANSWER: MAYBE. WHAT HAPPENS WHEN A BISON'S IN A BAD MOOD AND WANTS TO TAKE IT OUT ON A CAR? IN MOST CASES, THE BEAST ONLY BANGS UP THE CAR.

But an especially small car facing an especially big bison could probably wind up doorside down. So if you're ever in that situation and you see a bison paw the ground with its split hooves and put its huge, horned head down and its tail up—all signals that it's ready for action—you might want to brace yourself.

CREATURE FEATURES

American bison
Bison bison
Height: 6.5 feet (2 m) at the big hump over their shoulders
Weight: Up to 2,400 pounds (1,089 kg)
Location: Central and western Canada and parts of the western United States

CAN A BLUE WHALE EAT AN ELEPHANT?

WHAT DO WE KNOW?

Blue whales are the biggest animals on the planet . . . ever. If anything can eat an elephant, it would have to be a blue whale, right? Blue whales do eat an awful lot. In fact, a single blue whale can pack away as much as 4 tons (3.6 tonnes) of food every day. But it's a baleen whale, which means it doesn't have teeth.

ANSWER: NO. BLUE WHALES HAVE A HUGE APPETITE, BUT THEY COULDN'T EAT AN ELEPHANT.

The weight of food they eat each day is about the weight of a medium-size African elephant, so maybe the question wasn't actually so silly. But the thing is, a blue whale can eat only very small things: mostly krill. These are 2 inch (5 cm) shrimplike crustaceans. Snacking on such tiny things one at a time would take forever, so a blue whale grabs them in bulk. It takes a giant mouthful of water, closes its jaws, and forces the water back out, through sheets of bristles called baleen that hang from the top of its mouth. The krill are too big to fit through the baleen. (It's like a comb catching crumbs in your hair. Okay, that's gross. Just how are you eating, anyway?) The whale swallows the krill and then goes back for more.

WHAAAT?!

A blue whale's call can be heard underwater for thousands of miles.

CREATURE FEATURES

Blue whale
Balaenoptera musculus
Length: Up to 100 feet (30.5 m)
Weight: Up to 200 tons (that's 400,000 pounds, or 181,437 kg!)
Location: Oceans around the world

DOES LIVING IN THE DESERT GO TO A CAMEL'S HEAD?

WHAT DO WE KNOW?

Everything about a camel is perfectly made for life in the hot, desolate desert. (We're talking about dromedaries, or Arabian, camels here. The one-hump kind.) Starting at the top, camels have long eyelashes, membranes over their eyes, and nostrils that close up—all features that keep sand out. Their famous humps are for fat storage. When times are tough, and there's not enough food and water, camels tap into their humps. Their systems break down the fat stores there to make water and energy. Speaking of eating and drinking, camels can last a really, really long time without eating and drinking. It's hard to believe, but these desert dwellers can last a week without water and months without food. (They only sweat when it gets really hot.) And they can walk 20 miles (32 km) in a day (even carrying heavy loads) on broad, flat feet that make walking on sand easy.

ANSWER: ABSOLUTELY!

Living in the desert has gone to camels' heads, to their feet, to their bellies. It has gone to their whole bodies.

CREATURE FEATURES

Dromedary camel
Camelus dromedarius
Height: Up to 7 feet (2 m) at the hump
Weight: Up to 1,600 pounds (726 kg)
Location: The northern half of Africa, the Arabian Peninsula, and Central Asia

WHAAAT?!

Camels can drink around 30 gallons (114 l) of water in 13 minutes! That's enough to fill up a good-size home aquarium.

HOW CAN YOU USE A CARIBOU FOR A CALENDAR?

WHAT DO WE KNOW?

In the winter, male caribou shed their old antlers and start growing their new ones in early spring. (They grow a new set of antlers every year.) Caribou hooves become harder and sharper in winter, too, to help the animals walk in snow and break through ice to reach food. The animals' winter coats are lighter-colored. In winter, a caribou's tapetum, a layer at the back of some animals' eyes, is blue. Females start growing their antlers in late spring. In the summer, a caribou's tapetum turns gold, and the caribou grow darker coats. When winter comes again, the males' antlers drop.

ANSWER: CARIBOU, ALSO CALLED REINDEER, CHANGE IN VARIOUS WAYS THROUGHOUT THE YEAR.

If you had no calendar (and no ability to check the internet or even look out the window), and you wanted to know what time of year it was, if you had a caribou—which you probably do—you'd have all the information you needed.

WHAAAT?!

Antlers are made of bone. Caribou antlers, which are the largest of any deer compared to body size, can be 50 inches (1.3 m) long.

CREATURE FEATURES

Caribou
Rangifer tarandus
Height: Up to 5 feet (1.5 m) at the shoulder
Weight: Up to 700 pounds (318 kg)
Location: Far north regions around the world

COULD A CHEETAH EVER LOSE A RACE TO A HUMAN?

WHAT DO WE KNOW?

Cheetahs are natural-born sprinters, and they're the fastest animals on land. They can beat a horse handily. A cheetah can hit the 70-mile-per-hour (113 kmh) mark. Cheetahs, with their flexible spines, lightweight heads, and slender builds, are speed machines. Other predators count on strength or stealth. But cheetahs go fast or go home. In fact, when they're chasing dinner, like gazelles, rabbits, and ostriches, they need to knock down their prey in the first few hundred yards. Soon after that, the cheetah needs to stop and catch its breath for about 20 minutes.

ANSWER: IT DEPENDS ON THE RACE.

In a short race, a cheetah would win easily. The top speed ever reached by a human is 27.8 miles per hour (45 kmh). That was Usain Bolt during a 100-meter dash in 2009. The cheetah would've blasted by him at 70 mph (113 kmh).

But over a long race—say, a 5K—a human runner could beat the cheetah every time.

CREATURE FEATURES

Cheetah
Acinonyx jubatus
Length: Up to 7.5 feet (2.3 m)
Weight: Up to 140 pounds (63.5 kg)
Location: Mostly central and southern Africa

WHAT'S IN A CHIMPANZEE'S TOOLBOX?

WHAT DO WE KNOW?

We like to say humans are nature's great toolmakers, but chimps are surprisingly skilled when it comes to making and using tools. Maybe you've heard about chimps stripping off the leaves from thin sticks and then slipping the sticks inside termite mounds so they can pull out a bunch of tasty treats clinging to them. But chimps do so much more to turn the world around them into tools.

ANSWER: LOTS OF THINGS!

They use special rocks as hammers and anvils so they can crack open nuts. They use leaves as napkins and as sponges to soak up drinking water. They use long sticks as hunting spears and as "fishing rods" to scoop up algae and drag it out of the water. They use tiny sticks to dig marrow from bones. They use rocks as projectile weapons. They build nests from branches and leaves. Chimps even have different cultures—different groups of chimps use tools in different ways, and the youngsters learn these tricks from their mothers.

WHAAAT?!

Like humans, chimps are right- or left-handed.

CREATURE FEATURES

Chimpanzee
Pan troglodytes
Height: Up to 5.5 feet (1.7 m)
Weight: Up to 130 pounds (59 kg)
Location: Central Africa

ARE COYOTES GOOD NEIGHBORS?

WHAT DO WE KNOW?

Some animals are specialists—they live in very specific places and eat very specific foods. Think giant pandas eating nothing but bamboo all day long. (And read about pandas on page 102 of this book.) And then there are animals like coyotes. These smaller cousins of wolves can live just about anywhere and eat just about anything. You can find them in forests, mountains, and prairies. They'll happily chow down on mice, rabbits, squirrels, snakes, grass, fruit, frogs, and bugs. They'll also move in closer to people and live in suburbs and cities, where they can eat garden plants, pet food, and even . . . pets.

ANSWER: NO, IT DOESN'T SOUND LIKE COYOTES ARE GOOD NEIGHBORS.

But they are increasingly common neighbors. People often don't like it, but coyote populations are increasing in many places. You might even have some coyote neighbors you don't know about.

CREATURE FEATURES

Coyote
Canis latrans
Length: Up to 4.5 feet (1.4 m)
Weight: Up to 50 pounds (22.7 kg)
Location: Most of North America

DO DOLPHINS NEED THEIR BEAUTY SLEEP?

WHAT DO WE KNOW?

Dolphins are sleek and graceful, no question. So what's their secret? They eat well (a big bottlenose dolphin eats more than 80 pounds, or 36 kg, of fish a day) and get plenty of exercise (and they can reach speeds of more than 25 miles, or 45 kmh). We also know dolphins can go long stretches with no sleep. Newborn bottlenose dolphins and orcas—which are actually giant dolphins—stay awake for their whole first month! In experiments with bottlenose dolphins, scientists learned that the dolphins were still alert and capable of performing complex tasks (with 99 percent accuracy) even after 15 sleepless days. (One of the researchers called dolphins "unwavering sentinels of the sea," which is cool.)

ANSWER: NO, DOLPHINS DON'T NEED A TON OF SLEEP, LET ALONE BEAUTY SLEEP.

When dolphins do sleep, they go about it in a unique way: they sleep with half of their brains at a time. That way, dolphins can stay safe—remaining aware of their surroundings, watching for prey, and surfacing regularly to breathe.

CREATURE FEATURES

Bottlenose dolphin
Tursiops truncatus
Length: Up to 14 feet (4.3 m)
Weight: Up to 1,400 pounds (635 kg)
Location: Tropical and temperate waters around the world

WHAT IF AN ELEPHANT BUMPED INTO A CACTUS?

WHAT DO WE KNOW?

Elephants are powerhouses. They're the biggest land animals in the world, and they are incredibly strong. On the African savanna, elephants often knock down trees more than a foot thick so they can easily get at the nutritious leaves. They do need to work at it—pressing their faces against the tree and shoving and rocking it until it snaps and falls.

Elephants are famous for their thick skin. (It can be an inch thick—2.5 cm—in places.) But in some spots on an elephant's face and head, the skin is much thinner. And elephant skin is also sensitive. (Elephants are even susceptible to sunburn and use sand and dirt as a natural sunscreen.)

ANSWER: THE CACTUS PROBABLY WOULDN'T STAND A CHANCE, BUT IT'S A SAFE BET THAT AN ELEPHANT WOULD WIND UP WITH SOME CACTUS SPINES EMBEDDED IN ITS HIDE. OUCH.

CREATURE FEATURES

African elephant
Loxodonta africana
Height: Up to 13 feet (4 m) at the shoulder
Weight: Up to 14,000 pounds (6,350 kg)
Location: Much of Africa

WHAAAT?!

African elephants have two "fingers"—muscular little nubs—on the ends of their trunks. They use them for "handling" small objects.

COULD AN EMPEROR TAMARIN WIN A BEAUTY CONTEST?

WHAT DO WE KNOW?

Emperor tamarins are little gray-brown monkeys. These guys eat just about everything—flowers, frogs, bugs, eggs, and sap. Their small size lets them creep up on prey and reach fruit growing *waaaay* out on small branches. They're recognizable by their long and lavish, dapper and drooping white moustaches—on males *and* females. But what should also not go unnoticed is that these guys are playful and affectionate. In their social groups all adults help care for the children, and emperor tamarin dads are especially attentive, giving the youngsters more attention than the moms do.

ANSWER: WHAT KIND OF BEAUTY CONTEST ARE WE TALKING ABOUT HERE?

If it's some kind of old-timey moustache contest (like the annual and actually real World Beard and Moustache Championships®), emperor tamarins would have a good shot at an award.

CREATURE FEATURES

 Emperor tamarin
Saguinus imperator
Length: Up to 2.5 feet (0.8 m), including the tail
Weight: Up to 1 pound (0.5 kg)
Location: Northwest South America

WHAT IF A FENNEC FOX HAD, YOU KNOW, REGULAR EARS?

WHAT DO WE KNOW?

It's hard to imagine a fennec fox without those wonderfully oversized ears. If a fennec fox had more standard ears it would hardly even be able to fennec! That's because fennec foxes live in hot, sandy places, like the Sahara Desert. And those giant ears—they can be almost half the length of their bodies—let the foxes do two very crucial things: find food they can't see and radiate heat. A lot of what fennec foxes eat lives underground. And being able to hear insects and reptiles scrabbling around below the sand is totally necessary. Living in such a hot place also means you need to be able to keep your cool. Fennec foxes do that with giant ears that serve as reverse solar panels, sort of. They make it easy for the little animals to release heat from their bodies. Fennecs also dig deep burrows to stay out of the sun and have hairy soles on their feet to make it easier to walk on hot sand.

ANSWER: THAT FENNEC FOX WOULD BE PRETTY HUNGRY AND HOT.

CREATURE FEATURES

Fennec fox
Vulpes zerda
Length: Up to 2.5 feet (0.8 m), including tail
Weight: Up to 3.5 pounds (1.6 kg)
Location: Northern Africa and the Arabian Peninsula

ARE GIANT PANDAS AND RED PANDAS COUSINS?

WHAT DO WE KNOW?

Well, they both have the word *panda* in their names. Even if you ignore the names, there are some big similarities: Red pandas and giant pandas both love their bamboo. (Red pandas don't eat quite so much of it, and they're much pickier about which parts they eat.) And reds and giants both have that weird extra "thumb." (Read about giant pandas on page 102 of this book.) And they're both adorable!

ANSWER: IT'S EASY TO THINK THEY MUST BE. BUT NO!

Red pandas and giant pandas aren't closely related. Scientists have changed their minds about this many times over the years. They used to think red pandas belonged in the raccoon family, then in the bear family. Now they're believed to be in *their own* family. Wherever they fit on the tree of life, red pandas are pretty special. Long, puffy tails help them balance on branches, and special foot bones let them climb down trees headfirst. And red pandas are the only carnivores* with a special gland for letting them test certain odors.

CREATURE FEATURES

Red panda
Ailurus fulgens
Length: Up to 4 feet (1.2 m)
Weight: 14 pounds (6 kg)
Location: Nepal, Burma, and China

WHAAAT?!

Red pandas leave a scent with their feet. Humans can't smell it.

*Red pandas are mostly vegetarian, but they belong to the order Carnivora (which includes cats, dogs, bears, seals, weasels, etc.), so technically they're vegetarian carnivores.

WHAAAT?!

Giraffes' skulls grow thicker as they age to protect them when they headbutt other giraffes.

CAN GIRAFFES DUNK?

WHAT DO WE KNOW?

Let's start with the obvious: Giraffes are tall. Your average giraffe is around 16 feet (4.9 m) tall, so they could get to the hoop no problem at all. (A regulation basketball rim is 10 feet, or 3 m, off the ground.) Giraffes are also fast, capable of reaching a speed of around 35 miles (56 km) per hour, perfect for racing up and down the court. They have long necks, too. Male giraffes use them to spar with other males. And while these shoving matches don't usually get too violent, you can imagine how much raw power giraffes can generate with those sturdy, muscular necks.

ANSWER: NO, BECAUSE THEY COULDN'T PICK UP THE BALL.

But *could* they dunk, if they figured out how to hold a basketball—maybe by wrapping their gigantic tongues around it? Absolutely. Giraffes have everything else good basketball players need.

CREATURE FEATURES

Giraffe
Giraffa camelopardalis
(new research suggests there are four distinct giraffe species)
Height: Up to 19 feet (5.8 m)
Weight: Up to 3,000 pounds (1,361 kg)
Location: Central and southern Africa

DO GOATS NEED DENTURES?

WHAT DO WE KNOW?

Goats are browsers. That means they don't stand still and eat grass, but instead they like eating leaves and branches from trees and bushes, as well as wood-like weeds. On a farm, where they may not be able to browse, goats can eat up to 4 pounds (1.8 kg) of hay every day. With all of this chewing on hard material, you may think they have some hefty teeth. But actually . . .

ANSWER: NO. GOATS HAVE NO TOP TEETH AT ALL! BUT THEY STILL DON'T NEED DENTURES.

Instead of front top chompers, goats have something called a browsing pad, which looks like thick, toothless gums. This might sound inefficient for crunching away on branches, but the lack of top teeth actually lets them cram more tough stuff into their mouth, which they then mash against the dental pad. Goats also have four—yes, *four*—stomachs that help them digest their woody meals.

CREATURE FEATURES

Goat
Gazella dorcas
Height: 21–25 inches (53–64 cm)
Weight: 33–43 pounds (15–20 kg)
Location: Domesticated worldwide

WHY DON'T GOPHERS USE LUNCHBOXES?

WHAT DO WE KNOW?

Gophers are large rodents that are known for their tunneling abilities. They create large tunnel systems up to 3 feet (0.9 m) below ground, with a straight main section and lots of offshoots. Gophers spend lots of time underground, and they're well adapted for life under the dirt. They have four really large, strong teeth, which help them burrow. Their lips actually close behind their teeth, so they don't get mouthfuls of mud while they dig.

ANSWER: BECAUSE THEY CARRY THEIR FOOD IN SPECIAL CHEEK POCKETS.

That's right. Gophers have fur-lined pockets in their cheeks, which they can access through little holes in their furry faces. Why not carry the food in their mouths? Because if they did, the seeds and roots that they eat would soak up their saliva and leave them needing more water. So into the chubby little cheeks the food goes.

CREATURE FEATURES

Gopher or pocket gopher
38 species in the family Geomyidae
Height: 4–14 inches (10–36 cm)
Weight: 1–2 pounds (0.5–0.9 kg)
Location: In North American from Southern Canada to Northwestern Colombia

WHAT WOULD HAPPEN IF A GORILLA WENT TO THE GYM?

WHAT DO WE KNOW?

Many of the estimates of gorillas' and other nonhuman primates' strength are probably not very scientific. One thing everyone agrees on is that gorillas are way stronger than us humans, possibly 6 times stronger. Some people estimate that a gorilla can lift 10 times its body weight. (The strongest humans in the world can lift about 3 times their body weight.) Gorillas can break tree branches and easily move heavy objects that humans can hardly shift at all—even with the help of a couple of friends. Another thing gorilla researchers will tell you is that gorillas are generally calm and peaceful animals. Even the biggest, toughest silverbacks—older males who lead family groups—tend to save their aggressive displays for times when something threatens the troop. And when that happens, look out. An angry silverback will smack the ground, rear up, pound his chest, hoot, and charge! And if the silverback had been spending time at the gym . . .

ANSWER: A GORILLA COULD PROBABLY LEARN TO USE ALL KINDS OF GYM EQUIPMENT, LIKE DUMBBELLS AND WEIGHT MACHINES, BUT THEN WHAT?

Well, gorillas are already superstrong, so after working out, a gorilla would be super-superstrong.

CREATURE FEATURES

Gorilla

2 species in the genus *Gorilla*

Height: Up to 6 feet (1.8 m)

Weight: Up to 485 pounds (220 kg)

Location: Central Africa

ARE GRIZZLY BEARS LONELY?

WHAT DO WE KNOW?

Except for mothers and their cubs, grizzlies spend most of their time by themselves. When they gather in large numbers, it's only at prime fishing spots, where many bears congregate to swipe salmon from rivers during their upstream summer migrations. Speaking of which, that's what bears spend a lot of their waking lives doing: finding food. And they find it everywhere. They eat parts of hundreds of different plants, rodents, elk, and moose, among other things. All this eating lets them pack on the pounds to prep for the long, deep sleep of hibernation. Grizzlies hibernate for as much as half the year. (And that's more "alone time"!) In general, the farther north a bear lives, the longer it hibernates. During hibernation, a grizzly's system slows way down. It might breathe only once or twice a minute, and its heart can beat as few as eight times a minute.

ANSWER: NO. THEY'RE PROBABLY NOT LONELY, BUT THEY'RE OFTEN ALONE.

WHAAAT?!

Don't believe the rumors: grizzlies can run uphill *and* downhill.

CREATURE FEATURES

 Grizzly bear
Ursus arctos horribilis
(grizzlies are a subspecies of brown bear)
Length: Up to 9 feet (2.7 m)
Weight: Up to 900 pounds (408 kg)
Location: Northwestern North America

IF HEDGEHOGS WERE AS TALL AS US, WOULD THEY RULE THE WORLD?

WHAT DO WE KNOW?

Just for a minute, forget everything you know about hedgehogs, and pretend you're hearing about them for the first time. (Ready?) There's this monster whose back is covered with thousands of sharp, crisscrossing spines. This beast can curl up into a spiky ball so tight that prying it apart is more than most predators can handle. They are immune to the toxins of many plants and the venom of many snakes! They even eat poisonous plants, foam at the mouth, and rub the saliva on their spines for extra dangerousness! They can live in all kinds of climates—from desert to forest. They have even been known to stalk the streets of *human cities*, grunting horribly as they go. They can dig like crazy, and they have excellent hearing. Can nothing stop them? Are we at their mercy? Well, we definitely would be if they weren't usually just a few inches long and about the cutest things on the planet.

CREATURE FEATURES

Hedgehog
17 species in the family
Erinaceidae
Length: Up to 12 inches
(30 cm)
Weight: Up to 3.5 pounds
(1.6 kg)
Location: Africa, Europe, and Asia

ANSWER: YES. YES, THEY WOULD.

DOES A HIPPO USE SUNSCREEN?

WHAT DO WE KNOW?

Hippos are like beach bums, spending lots of time lazing in the water. (*Hippopotamus* means "river horse," after all, so it's no surprise they like catching some waves and soaking up rays.) Hippos love the water, but they don't float. Instead, they walk on river bottoms. They keep their heads underwater and can hold their breath for 5 minutes. Hippos need to keep their skin moist in their hot climates. But don't let all this lazy beach-talk fool you: hippos are among the most aggressive mammals alive. And they've got the bulk and the bite to back it up.

ANSWER: YES, ALL THE TIME.

Actually, they *make their own* sunscreen, and it's deluxe. It has germ-killing properties that might prevent infections. Known sometimes as "blood sweat" (ew), this thick, red goop coats the hippo and protects it from the sun. Don't worry, it's not actually blood. It's not actually sweat either, but it oozes from the hippos' skin the same way sweat does. At first, it's colorless, but as it reacts with sunlight, it becomes red.

WHAAAT?!

A hippo's canine teeth can be almost 2 feet (0.6 m) long! That's bigger than a T. rex tooth!

CREATURE FEATURES

Common hippopotamus
Hippopotamus amphibius
Length: Up to 14 feet (4.3 m)
Weight: Up to 8,000 pounds (3,629 kg)
Location: Throughout central and southern Africa

IS IT TRUE THAT HONEY BADGERS JUST DON'T CARE?

WHAT DO WE KNOW?

Honey badgers will brave a hive full of bees just for a taste of the baby bees (or brood) inside. And while their tough, loose skin is hard for bees to sting (and for porcupines to stick with quills and for dogs to puncture with teeth), a whole swarm of bees working together can drive a honey badger back. Honey badgers have even been found dead beside beehives. That's right: not even the threat of death is enough to make them think twice about eating that bee brood. These critters will snarl at leopards (clearly way, way bigger and stronger) and chase and chow down on venomous snakes. The toxins don't kill them. Snakes are just another annoyance in a honey badger's wild life.

CREATURE FEATURES

Honey badger (also called a ratel)
Mellivora capensis
Length: Up to 4 feet (1.2 m)
Weight: Up to 30 pounds (13.6 kg)
Location: Much of Africa, the Middle East, Central Asia, and India

ANSWER: YES, INDEED IT IS.

They really don't care. Honey badgers have been called the world's most fearless animal, so you know they didn't earn their name from being sweet and gentle. (Ha!) No, the name comes from their love of honey.

WHAT DOES A HOUSE CAT SEE IN A PITCH-BLACK ROOM?

WHAT DO WE KNOW?

Cats have remarkably good night vision. They need much less light than we do. Retinas (the light-sensitive layer of cells at the back of the eye) have rod cells (for seeing in low light) and cone cells (for seeing color). Cats have far more rods and fewer cones than we do. This means they can see very well at night, but they can't tell red and green apart. It's a trade-off: they can hunt in (not quite total) darkness but have no fashion sense at all. A cat's eye also has a slit pupil, which is different from yours, which is round, and this pupil can open very wide at night, to let in lots of light. And a layer of reflective cells behind a cat's retina makes it even more sensitive to light.

ANSWER: IF THE ROOM IS PITCH-BLACK, CATS SEE THE SAME THING YOU SEE: NOTHING AT ALL. ALL EYES—EVEN THE MOST SENSITIVE EYES—NEED SOME LIGHT TO SEE BY.

Okay, fine. So in a totally, completely, 100 percent dark room, a cat can't see anything. But, say, in your bedroom at night, the cat can see a lot more detail than you can.

CREATURE FEATURES

House cat (also called a domestic cat)
Felis catus
Length: Up to 2.5 feet (0.8 m)
Weight: Up to 20 pounds (9 kg)
Location: Everywhere humans live

The structure of a cat's eyes helps it see so well. Their pupils, or the black part of their eyes, can grow from narrow slits to big round circles. This allows them to take in more light than a human's eye can. They also have large lenses and their corneas—the clear part of the eyes—is big and curved. All of that helps them focus better.

WHAT IF *HUMANS* KEPT GROWING FOR THEIR ENTIRE LIVES?

WHAT DO WE KNOW?

Some animals—many snakes and lizards, for example—keep growing for their entire lives. And a rodent's teeth are always growing. But humans don't work that way. Except for hair, fingernails, and ears, we're usually done growing by the time we're in our early twenties.

ANSWER: HUMANS WOULD BE HUUUUGE IF WE KEPT GROWING AT THE SAME SUPERFAST RATE WE DID IN OUR FIRST YEAR.

If we grew taller at the same rate, we could be expect to be around 94 feet (29 m) tall when we celebrated our tenth birthdays. If you think that's amazing, think about this: we could expect to weigh more than 200 tons (181 tonnes). In scientific terms, this is, like, *whoa humongous*. If you kept growing at this rate, by the time you were 100 you'd be about 125 trillion *miles* (more than 201 trillion km) tall. That's about 21 light-years tall. A light-year is the distance light travels in 1 year. Put it this way: you could stand on Earth (well, you could if you weren't so huge) and touch one of the closest stars in the constellation Cassiopeia. And you would weigh close to a million times more than the entire Milky Way galaxy. It's probably a good thing people don't keep growing at that first-year rate for their whole lives. Where would we even buy clothes?

WHAAAT?!

If you didn't cut your hair, it could grow to around 5 feet (1.5 m) long by your tenth birthday, and your fingernails would be about 16 inches (41 cm) long if left uncut.

CREATURE FEATURES

Human
Homo sapiens sapiens
Height: 5.5 feet (1.7 m) on average
Weight: 180 pounds (82 kg) on average
Location: Worldwide

HOW DO YOU CATCH AN IMPALA?

WHAT DO WE KNOW?

Impalas aren't just waiting around for a big cat or a hyena to grab them. When an impala notices a predator—a lion, say—it will alert the herd, and they all take off. Impalas are fast, and they're agile. They can cover more than 30 feet (9.1 m) in a single leap, and they can jump 10 feet (3 m) high. If a lion doesn't catch an impala before the herd hears the alarm, they're not too likely to make a kill. (Lions are successful in about 20 percent of all attempts.) Besides speed and acrobatic skills, impalas also have good choices in friends. They are known to hang out with baboons. When the baboons snack on the fruits of the sausage tree (no, really), the impalas are there. And they get something out of the arrangement beyond scraps. They get to rely on the baboons as lookouts, too.

ANSWER: STEP 1: BE A LION. STEP 2: BE LUCKY.

If you can't manage steps 1 and 2, you might be out of luck.

CREATURE FEATURES

Impala
Aepyceros melampus
Height: Up to 3.5 feet
(1 m) at the shoulder
Weight: Up to 165 pounds
(75 kg)
Location: Southern Africa

WHAT WOULD HAPPEN IF A KANGAROO JUMPED ON A TRAMPOLINE?

WHAT DO WE KNOW?

They are perfectly built for their leaping lifestyle. The biggest kangaroos can cover 25 feet (7.6 m) in one bounce, and they can hit speeds of 35 miles (56 km) per hour. They owe their hopping ability to their tails. In effect, kangaroos are five-legged animals. Their tails supply as much power as their front and back legs combined. Also? When they're mad? They can prop themselves up on their tails and kick with their giant back feet.

ANSWER: BELIEVE IT OR NOT, KANGAROO-ON-TRAMPOLINE ISN'T A HYPOTHETICAL MATTER FOR PHILOSOPHERS TO ARGUE ABOUT. THIS HAS ACTUALLY HAPPENED. (WHAT A WORLD WE LIVE IN!)

So what do you think? Did the trampoline give the kangaroo double-jumping ability? Well, yes and no. The springy surface did seem to give the kangaroo's jump some extra oomph. But the kangaroo lost style points when it did an unintentional forward flip and ended up in the grass. It's just as well. Kangaroos don't need the extra help anyway.

CREATURE FEATURES

Red kangaroo
Macropus rufus
Height: Up to 6 feet
(1.8 m)
Weight: Up to 200 pounds
(91 kg)
Location: Much of
Australia

WHAT ARE HYENAS LAUGHING ABOUT ANYWAY?

WHAT DO WE KNOW?

Life on the African savanna is no joke for hyenas. They always have to keep one eye out for their archrivals: lions. Lions steal hyena kills (to be fair, hyenas steal lion kills, too) and even attack hyenas. Hyenas are tough and smart, and a hyena bite is incredibly strong. They hunt like wolves, working together as a pack to bring down large prey: wildebeests, impalas, zebras, and Cape buffalo calves, among others.

ANSWER: NOTHING AT ALL.

These yipping, giggling predator-scavengers are deadly serious. And all their famously funny-sounding calls are just their way of communicating—about themselves, about the clan, and about danger. They laugh and they grumble. They even kind of honk. Each member of a hyena clan has its own whoop. And cubs make a sound that hyena researchers call "squittering."

WHAAAT?!

Female hyenas are bigger than the males. And a single alpha female is in charge of the clan.

CREATURE FEATURES

Spotted hyena
Crocuta crocuta
Length: Up 6.5 feet (2 m)
Weight: Up to 180 pounds (82 kg)
Location: Central and southern Africa

DO KOALAS LIKE TO CHILL?

WHAT DO WE KNOW?

Nestled in a comfy spot in a eucalyptus tree, a koala will eat leaves at night—as many as 1.75 pounds (600 g) of leaves. That would be like you eating around 8 pounds (3.6 kg). And they *love* these leaves. They even keep some in their cheeks for snacking on later. In addition to being tasty (to koalas), eucalyptus leaves are tough and poisonous. A koala's extralong digestive tract with its special bacteria lets it break the leaves down safely. When koalas aren't eating or thinking about eating, they're sleeping. They can fit in 18 hours of sleep a day, easily. Koalas don't mess around with their sleeping and eating.

ANSWER: HA! ARE EUCALYPTUS LEAVES TOXIC? YES AND YES.

A koala's two favorite things to do are eating and sleeping. They're like the teenagers of the animal kingdom.

CREATURE FEATURES

Koala
Phascolarctos cinereus
Length: Up to 3 feet (0.9 m)
Weight: Up to 20 pounds (9 kg)
Location: Eastern Australia

WHAAAT?!

Koalas are usually relaxed and peaceful, but a disturbed koala can get aggressive and surly. Just like a teenager!

WHAT IF YOU BUILT A LEOPARD A TREE HOUSE?

WHAT DO WE KNOW?

Leopards are totally at home in the trees. From a perch high above the ground, they can rest, watch for prey, or eat a meal. Leopards are stalk-and-ambush hunters, relying on stealth and strength more than speed, although they're plenty fast. After making a kill, leopards will often drag the carcass into a tree and wedge it into a forked branch to keep it safe from hyenas and lions. Imagine hauling 150 pounds (68 kg) or more into a tree . . . with your mouth! Leopards also hunt from trees—dropping on top of prey, like impalas, to stun it. They can also hunt *in* the trees, chasing monkeys, birds, and even squirrels from branch to branch and from tree to tree. They are powerful hunters, and they will stop at nothing in their pursuit of prey. (They will even swim to hunt down crabs and fish.) If a leopard had a tree house, a well-equipped base of operation, and not just a branch to lie on and leaves to hide behind, just think what it could accomplish.

ANSWER: THEY'D LOVE YOU FOREVER.

CREATURE FEATURES

Leopard
Panthera pardus
Length: Up to 11 feet (3.4 m), including the tail
Weight: Up to 175 pounds (79 kg)
Location: Africa and Asia

DO LIONS WORK TOO HARD?

WHAT DO WE KNOW?

Lions live in groups called prides, which are groups made up of three to forty lions, with usually just a few males and many females. It's the females who do most of the hunting. Alone or in pairs or larger groups, lionesses work together to take down prey like antelope, zebras, wildebeests, and other large animals. These are big, fast creatures, so teamwork is crucial. After a kill, who comes along to eat first? The adult male lion (or lions) of the pride. When he's done, the lionesses get their turn. After that, it's time for the kids to eat what they can.

ANSWER: YES—IF YOU'RE TALKING ABOUT LIONESSES, THEY WORK TOO HARD. IF YOU'RE THINKING OF THE MALES, THEN NOT SO MUCH.

Why do the males get to laze around waiting for someone to ring the dinner bell? They're in charge of keeping the pride together and safe. They chase off intruders and fend off rival lions.

CREATURE FEATURES

Lion
Panthera leo
Length: Up to 10 feet (3 m), including the tail
Weight: Up to 420 pounds (190 kg)
Location: Central and southern Africa

ARE MANATEES WISHY-WASHY?

WHAT DO WE KNOW?

Manatees are water-dwelling mammals that are sometimes called sea cows. Some manatees switch habitats between freshwater and saltwater, hanging out in both environments. West Indian manatees, the largest species, prefer spots where freshwater and saltwater meet. Manatees have a special system that lets their kidneys filter out excess salt, so saltwater's no problem. Unlike other marine mammals, manatees don't have a thick layer of blubber. They need to stay in a warm environment. Throughout the year, they change their territory, always following the warm water. This could be places where warm rivers empty into the sea or even areas around power plants where warm water is discharged. When they're not eating, manatees spend most of their time near the surface. Their efficient lungs allow them to remain underwater for more than 15 minutes between breaths.

ANSWER: MAYBE. IN THE TYPICAL SENSE, *WISHY-WASHY* WOULD MEAN MANATEES HAVE TROUBLE MAKING DECISIONS. MANATEES MIGHT BE JUST THAT, SINCE THEY SPEND SO MUCH TIME MOVING BETWEEN ENVIRONMENTS—OR THEY'RE JUST LOOKING FOR NUTRIENT-RICH WARM WATER.

WHAAAT?!

Compared to body size, manatees have the smallest brains of any mammal. And their brains are smooth, not wrinkled.

CREATURE FEATURES

West Indian manatee
Trichechus manatus
Length: Up to 13 feet (4 m)
Weight: Up to 1,300 pounds (590 kg)
Location: Coastal waters of Central America, the Caribbean, and the south-eastern United States

WHAT IF A MEERKAT FAMILY ADOPTED YOU?

WHAT DO WE KNOW?

Meerkats live in mobs—*mob* is the word for a big group of meerkats living together. Most of the babies come from the dominant pair of meerkats, and there are a lot of them. Meerkats have different roles in the mob.

ANSWER: IF YOU WERE LUCKY ENOUGH TO BE WELCOMED INTO A MEERKAT MOB, YOU COULD EXPECT TO BE PUT TO WORK.

Meerkats are busy little things, and there's a lot to do. That means some meerkats are always on babysitter duty. And while the rest of the mob forages for food, someone needs to be on guard duty, watching for jackals and birds of prey. You'd need to learn the special lookout calls that mean "Everything's cool" and "Land predator!" and "Birds approaching! Run!" You might be asked to help beat up dangerous snakes that get too close to the mob's burrows. Speaking of which, you'd probably be off the hook when it comes to burrow digging. You (probably) don't have the long claws, special eye membranes, or close-up-able ears for it.

Being adopted by a meerkat family is not as out-there as it sounds. Meerkats have allowed (nonhuman) nonmeerkats to join their groups before. They've been known to share their burrows with squirrels and mongooses.

CREATURE FEATURES

Meerkat
Suricata suricatta
Length: Up to 2.5 feet (0.8 m), including the tail
Weight: Up to 2.2 pounds (1 kg)
Location: Southern Africa

WHAAAT?!

Researchers have filmed narwhals stunning fish by tapping them with the tips of their tusks before gobbling them up.

COULD A NARWHAL WIN A SWORD FIGHT?

WHAT DO WE KNOW?

Narwhals are toothed whales that have a long tusk. The tusk is really an incredible, flexible, spiraling tooth that grows right through the animal's face. It can be a mind-boggling 10 feet (3 m) long. Narwhal tusks are mostly a male thing—only a small percentage of females have them. They appear to be very sophisticated sensory organs. Thanks to the nerves packed inside and the many tiny holes in the surface of the tusk, the narwhal can collect lots of useful data about its surroundings: temperature, water pressure, and salinity (the saltiness of the water). By taking these readings, narwhals can learn about ocean conditions. Picking up on changes in salinity can alert a narwhal to the formation of ice, which can be a real hazard.

ANSWER: A SWORD FIGHT? AGAINST A PERSON HOLDING A SWORD AND SLASHING IT AROUND? SADLY, THAT'S UNLIKELY.

But! Narwhals do sometimes fight each other—or challenge each other or try to show off—with their tusks.

CREATURE FEATURES

Narwhal
Monodon monoceros
Length: Up to 16 feet (4.9 m) not including the tusk!
Weight: Up to 3,500 pounds (1,588 kg)
Location: Northern Atlantic and Arctic Oceans

HAS AN OPOSSUM EVER WON AN ACADEMY AWARD FOR ACTING?

WHAT DO WE KNOW?

When an opossum is in danger of attack, it might "play possum," putting on the most realistic show you ever saw. Here's the scene: A predator—say, a bobcat—has the opossum cornered. There's no escape. Its sharp, little teeth bared, the opossum goes still, like it's dead. It doesn't blink its eyes. Its breathing slows way down, so it's barely noticeable. It might drool or foam at the mouth. It might even let loose a terrible smell. The opossum stays like that for minutes or even *hours*. The act is so lifelike (deathlike?) that predators sometimes give up and walk off. It's like they forget that the opossum was clearly alive, hissing and backing away, just moments before.

ANSWER: NO, AND IT'S AN OUTRAGE!

In all of the animal kingdom there is no greater actor than the opossum.

WHAAAT?!

Opossums are also excellent at hanging on to branches with their tails when they climb, and they should win awards for that, too.

CREATURE FEATURES

Virginia opossum
Didelphis virginiana
Length: Up to 3.5 feet (1 m), including the tail
Weight: Up to 13.5 pounds (6.1 kg)
Location: Much of the United States, Mexico, and Central America

WOULD AN ORANGUTAN SPEAK HIS MIND?

WHAT DO WE KNOW?

In general, these tree-dwelling apes are solitary, coming together in large groups only when food is plentiful. So they spend a lot of time alone in the jungles of Borneo. They have large, round faces, and males have large, baggy throat sacs. Orangutans are also very strong.

ANSWER: THEY DO THROUGH VARIOUS FACIAL EXPRESSIONS AND THROUGH BODY LANGUAGE, AND BY MAKING CERTAIN SOUNDS AND CALLS. AND OCCASIONALLY BY THROWING TEMPER TANTRUMS.

Orangutans don't rely on their voices much, and they have a fairly limited "vocabulary." They make a kind of kissing sound, and males are well known for their loud, raspy hoots that can carry a long distance. These calls mean something like "I'm just passing through. Don't worry about me." The calls also let females know who's around. The males' flanges (also known as cheek pads) are wide ridges surrounding their faces, and some scientists think that they work like natural megaphones, making the calls louder. (It's the same effect as cupping your hands around your mouth when you want to be heard far away.) The males' throat sacs also up the volume of their calls. When orangutans see someone new, they sometimes shake branches and uproot dead trees.

CREATURE FEATURES

Orangutan
2 species in the genus
Pongo
Height: Up to 5 feet
(1.5 m)
Weight: Up to 200 pounds
(91 kg)
Location: Borneo

WHAAAT?!

An orangutan's arm spread can be 7 feet (2.1 m)!

DO ORCAS HAVE GOOD TABLE MANNERS?

WHAT DO WE KNOW?

Not only are orcas huge and powerful, but they're smart, too. They work together like a big, wet wolf pack. One of their favorite hunting techniques is a coordinated attack that washes a seal from an ice floe so they can easily eat it. A bunch of orcas will charge toward the floe at the same time, creating a big wave that sweeps the seal into the water and a lone orca waiting for it. Orcas will also lunge up onto the shore to snatch seals that thought they were safe out of the water. The orca grabs the seal, tosses it around, and then pulls it back into the water to eat.

ANSWER: NO. ORCAS HAVE TERRIBLE TABLE MANNERS!

And you can't trust them to wait until everyone's ready to start eating. If there are any seals lying around—even if you've labeled them with your name—orcas will swipe them. They go to great lengths to snatch seals in the wild.

WHAAAT?!

Orcas also herd and stun fish and drown much bigger whales. No prey is safe when orcas are around.

CREATURE FEATURES

Orca
Orcinus orca
Length: Up to 32 feet
(9.8 m)
Weight: Up to 6 tons
(5.4 tonnes)
Location: Worldwide

COULD A PANDA WIN A PIE-EATING CONTEST?

WHAT DO WE KNOW?

Pandas are famous for their amazing appetite for bamboo. Bamboo makes up almost 100 percent of their diet. (But it's true that they'll occasionally eat other foods if they're available: fruit, bugs, and even rodents.) Unfortunately, bamboo's not the best food source, which is why the pandas need to eat so much of it to get enough nutrition. That is why they spend more than 12 hours a day eating as much as 40 pounds (18 kg) of it. They plop themselves down in the mountains of China and chew up the inner stalks. They strip off the leaves, gather them in a bunch, and eat them. Pandas have a specialized "false thumb" (actually an enlarged wrist bone) that helps them hold and handle bamboo stalks. For pandas, it's all about the bamboo.

ANSWER: IT DEPENDS ON THE PIE.

If we're talking about regular pies—apple, cherry, blueberry— probably not. But if the pies in question are bamboo pies, a panda could easily walk away with first place.

CREATURE FEATURES

Giant panda
Ailuropoda melanoleuca
Length: Up to 5 feet (1.5 m)
Weight: Up to 300 pounds (136 kg)
Location: China

WHAAAT?!

There are fewer than 2,000 pandas left in the wild.

WHAT SHOULD YOU DO IF A PANGOLIN STICKS ITS TONGUE OUT AT YOU?

WHAT DO WE KNOW?

A pangolin's tongue can be more than a foot (30 cm) long, and it's sticky. Pangolins are special: they're among the only mammals with no teeth. But who needs teeth when you have a tongue perfectly built for slurping up bugs? Of course, it's not just the pangolin's tongue that's made for bug-eating. Pangolins have long, curved claws for tearing apart anthills and ripping bark from trees. And they can constrict special muscles to close up their ears and noses so bugs can't get in while they're feasting. If you were lucky enough to see a pangolin in the wild, you'd see a hunched-over creature walking on its hind legs, almost comically holding its little arms close to its body, covered head to toe in scales that resemble the petals of a pinecone. Pangolins can't see or hear well, but their noses work great for sniffing out dinner.

ANSWER: DUCK!

You really don't want to get in the way of a sticky pangolin tongue. True, unless you're an ant or a termite, the long, pink ribbon-y tongue won't hurt you, but it would still be kind of gross.

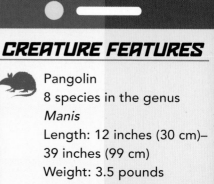

CREATURE FEATURES

Pangolin
8 species in the genus
Manis
Length: 12 inches (30 cm)–39 inches (99 cm)
Weight: 3.5 pounds (1.6 kg)–73 pounds (33 kg)

WHAT WOULD HAPPEN IF YOU BLINDFOLDED A PLATYPUS?

WHAT DO WE KNOW?

Platypuses, those famous hodgepodges of animal parts, hunt for at least 10 hours a day in the murky riverbeds of Australia. They sift through the stuff at the bottom of a river or go after individual shrimps, bugs, or worms. They keep the food in their cheek pouches until they're ready to hit the surface. They can stay underwater for about 2 minutes. When it's time to eat, they grind everything up between tough plates. That's right: no teeth!

ANSWER: BESIDES ANNOYING THE POOR THING? PROBABLY NOT MUCH.

Platypuses do all their best work with their big, rubbery bills. During all that time they spend hunting, they don't even use their eyes and ears. They close them up, along with their nostrils, and go on "nose feel." Their bills are very sensitive and appear to pick up electrical signals, too, similar to the way a shark's special receptors do. (Read about sharks on pages 27 and 28 of this book.)

CREATURE FEATURES

Platypus
Ornithorhynchus anatinus
Length: Up to 2 feet (0.6 m)
Weight: Up to 7 pounds (3.2 kg)
Location: Eastern Australia

WHAAAT?!

Platypuses are so unusual that European scientists first thought they weren't even real.

ARE POLAR BEARS WHITE?

WHAT DO WE KNOW?

Finally! A simple question! Of course polar bears are white. Apart from their eyes and noses, they're completely white (okay, and maybe a little yellowish sometimes) so they can blend in with the snow. Next question!

ANSWER: WAIT A SEC, WAIT A SEC. NO, POLAR BEARS ONLY APPEAR WHITE.

For one thing, their skin is black, to absorb as much heat as possible. Every bit helps when you live in the Arctic. But their fur isn't actually white either. The hairs in a polar bear's pelt are actually hollow and colorless. They are filled with air, which provides insulation from the cold. They also have a layer of blubbery fat for further protection from freezing conditions. All that fat also helps them stay afloat when they go swimming, which they do very well. Polar bears are the largest carnivores on land, and they are excellent hunters. They can sniff out prey from miles away.

CREATURE FEATURES

Polar bear
Ursus maritimus
Length: Up to 8 feet (2.4 m)
Weight: Up to 1,600 pounds (726 kg)
Location: The Arctic and as far south as Hudson Bay, Canada

MORE POLAR BEAR STATS

Polar bears . . .

. . . are the BIGGEST meat-eaters on Earth.

. . . can swim very far— some have been found more than 200 miles (370 km) from the nearest shore.

. . . number about 20,000 in the wild.

. . . are born one at a time or in pairs, and the cubs stay with their moms for about 2 years.

WHAAAT?!

Polar bears are powerful watch-and-wait predators. They scope out seal breathing holes and wait for seals to pop up.

COULD A PORCUPINE SHOOT ITS QUILLS THROUGH A BULLETPROOF VEST?

WHAT DO WE KNOW?

The back of the North American porcupine (there are more than 20 porcupine species in the Americas, Europe, Africa, and Asia) is covered with 30,000 quills. Quills are modified hairs about 3 inches (7.6 cm) long. Each porcupine quill is tipped with a sharp, backward-pointing barb. When a predator such as a fisher (a kind of weasel) gets too close, the porcupine turns around and lashes its tail, an unmistakable sign to back off. North American porcupines also make a distinct odor—predators that have had painful encounters with a porcupine will get the message and leave to go find an easier meal.

CREATURE FEATURES

North American porcupine
Erethizon dorsatum
Length: Up to 3 feet (0.9 m)
Weight: Up to 20 pounds (9 kg)
Location: Much of North America

ANSWER: NO, BUT . . .

A porcupine can't even shoot its quills through a sheet of paper. Porcupines can't shoot their quills at all, but they're still very effective defensive weapons. If you touch a porcupine, quills are likely to detach and come off in your flesh, and they burrow into skin.

DO QUOKKAS THINK WE'RE AS CUTE AS WE THINK THEY ARE?

WHAT DO WE KNOW?

With their perma-smiles and big, black noses, they seem like the sweetest little creatures in the world. But quokkas are tougher than they appear. Thanks to special adaptations allowing them to endure periods of drought, they can go long periods without food and water. The sturdy little things are not usually aggressive, but males have been known to squabble with one another on hot days over the best spots to hide from the sun. They're active during the night, coming out to feed in large groups more than 100 quokkas strong.

ANSWER: NO, DOESN'T SEEM POSSIBLE, DOES IT? JUST LOOK AT THEM!

Even if they don't think we're as cute as we think they are, what do they think of people? Well, they're not scared of us, that's for sure. Quokkas are known to approach humans with bold curiosity, looking for handouts (and sometimes maybe just friendship). If a quokka comes begging, don't give in. People food isn't good for these grass-and-leaf-eating marsupials. (Also, they can bite. Also, it's against the law to touch them.)

CREATURE FEATURES

Quokka
Setonix brachyurus
Length: Up to 3 feet (0.9 m), including the long, hairless tail
Weight: Up to 9.5 pounds (4.3 kg)
Location: Southwestern Australia

WOULD A RACCOON DO THE DISHES?

WHAT DO WE KNOW?

Raccoons like to forage at night, and they'll eat fruit, nuts, bugs, small rodents, frogs, crayfish, and eggs. Raccoons living around people will dine on pet food and stuff they find in garbage cans, too. Raccoons are famous for eating just about anything *and* for washing their food, so maybe it makes sense to think they'd combine the two and wash your dishes. (Maybe.)

ANSWER: NO. TRUTH TIME: RACCOONS DON'T ACTUALLY WASH THEIR FOOD.

Yes, they often dunk their food in water, but it's not because they're washing it. And it's not because they don't make saliva and therefore need to soften their food, like some people say. It's because they are used to finding food in water, and their dexterous little hands are even more sensitive in water. So when they stick food in water and appear to wash it off, they're actually examining it to "see" what they're eating.

CREATURE FEATURES

Common raccoon
Procyon lotor
Length: Up to 3.5 feet (1 m), including the tail
Weight: Up to 23 pounds (10.4 kg)
Location: North and South America

WHAAAT?!

Raccoons living way up north sleep inside their dens for most of the winter.

WHAT'S A DAY AT THE RHINO SPA LIKE?

WHAT DO WE KNOW?

Rhinos love to wallow (to roll around in watery mud). They do it to cool down and to protect their skin from the sun and from biting bugs. Rhinos are very territorial, and they mark their turf with giant piles of poop. But some good wallowing spots are no-fighting zones: anyone is welcome.

ANSWER: THE FIRST THING YOU NEED TO KNOW IS THAT YOU MIGHT HAVE TROUBLE MAKING AN APPOINTMENT, ON ACCOUNT OF ALL THE WALLOWING.

Rhinos do it for hours, so there may not be room for you at the spa. They also enjoy the attention of the spa's hardest-working employees: oxpecker birds. These birds groom the rhinos, eating the ticks and other parasites that bother them. They also serve as alarms. If danger approaches, the birds let the rhinos know. Still, you'd need to be careful. Rhinos are known for their massive bulk *and* for their bad eyesight. Because their vision is so poor, they often charge things they're unsure of. Are you sure you want to visit this spa?

WHAAAT?!

Oxpecker birds can reach all the way inside a rhino's big ears to find bugs.

CREATURE FEATURES

Rhino
5 species in the family Rhinocerotidae
Length: 10 feet (3 m)–13 feet (4 m), depending on the species
Weight: 1,800 pounds (816 kg)–5,000 pounds (2,268 kg), depending on the species
Location: Africa and southern Asia

HOW DO SEA LIONS COOL OFF?

WHAT DO WE KNOW?

Sea lions are related to seals and walruses—they're all part of a group of animals called pinnipeds, which means "wing-footed." This group of animals uses their wing-feet, or flippers, for maneuvering underwater and, a little less gracefully, on land.

ANSWER: WHEN SEA LIONS NEED MORE COOLING THAN A DIP IN THE OCEAN CAN PROVIDE, THEY USE THEIR FLIPPERS.

It's the same as elephants using their ears and toucans using their beaks to regulate temperature (read about toucans on page 23 of this book). The many blood vessels near the surface of a sea lion's flippers make them good spots for radiating excess heat. In fact, on very hot days, you might see a whole bunch of sea lion flippers sticking out of the water like a line of wet flags. This is sea lions cooling off. Their flippers work the other way, too. When it's very cold, those little blood vessels constrict to conserve heat.

CREATURE FEATURES

Sea lion
6 species in the family Otariidae
Length: Up to 11 feet (3.3 m), depending on the species
Weight: Up to 2,200 pounds (998 kg), depending on the species
Location: Coastal waters of the Pacific Ocean

WHAAAT?!

When they're underwater, sea lions' noses close up, and some sea lions slow their heartbeats way down to use up oxygen more slowly.

WHAT DOES A SEA OTTER WANT FOR ITS BIRTHDAY?

WHAT DO WE KNOW?

It's all part of the sea otter's easygoing lifestyle. Sea otters spend a lot of time floating on their backs, wrapped up in giant seaweed called kelp, and grooming themselves. Unlike other marine mammals, sea otters don't have a layer of blubber to keep them warm. Instead, they have incredibly thick coats that must always be kept clean so they can provide good insulation. Sea otters also eat a lot—up to 16 pounds (7 kg) of food each day. And they eat lots of things: urchins, mussels, abalone, snails, crab, you name it.

ANSWER: SEA OTTERS WANT THE SAME THING MANY OF US WANT FOR OUR BIRTHDAYS: A SPECIAL ROCK!

Sea otters enjoy rocks for a good reason. You might've already guessed it: Since all of their favorite foods are hard-shelled or, in the case of a sea urchin, spiky, they need tools to help them crack open dinner. Sea otters use rocks to bash abalone shells and dislodge them from the seafloor. They also place rocks on their chests and smash mollusks against them. You can see how important a sea otter's special rock can be. Sea otters have a pocket under each front leg, a little place inside the baggy skin there. You'll never guess what they keep there. That's right: their favorite rocks.

WHAAAT?!

Two sea otters will often hold "hands" while sleeping, so they don't drift apart.

CREATURE FEATURES

Sea otter
Enhydra lutris
Length: Up to 4 feet (1.2 m)
Weight: Up to 65 pounds (29.5 kg)
Location: Coastal areas of the northern Pacific Ocean

ARE SKUNKS ACTUALLY LITTLE STINKERS?

WHAT DO WE KNOW?

These little guys have powerfully smelly sprays that are legendary. If a skunk is mad at you or frightened, it will raise its tail, turn away from you, and let loose with a well-aimed spray from as far away as 10 feet (3 m). (Some species of skunk even do handstands when they spray.) The horrible stuff can be very hard to get off and can stay on a poor predator for days. But a skunk's coloring seems to point to its rear end, helpfully (and honestly) indicating the true source of its power. Look at the badger, another black animal with white stripes. A badger's stripes point toward its biting teeth. In fact, scientists say this kind of pattern is common: stripes often point to the animal's main attack, so predators know what they're in for.

ANSWERS: OF COURSE, IF WE MEAN IN THE SENSE OF "SMELLING REALLY, REALLY TERRIBLE."

If we take it to mean "Are skunks sneaky little cheaters?" we have to answer no—they're honestly advertising that they're stinky!

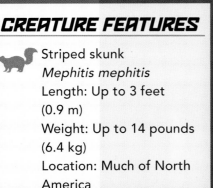

CREATURE FEATURES

Striped skunk
Mephitis mephitis
Length: Up to 3 feet (0.9 m)
Weight: Up to 14 pounds (6.4 kg)
Location: Much of North America

WHAAAT?!

Zorillas, stinky sprayers that live in Africa, are not closely related to skunks, but they have the same tail-highlighting stripes!

WHY DID THE SLOTH CROSS THE ROAD?

WHAT DO WE KNOW?

These total slowpokes spend very little time on the ground, where they have a tough time getting around, because their back legs are practically useless on the ground. In fact, they spend most of their lives way up high in the trees, upside down, coming down to poop about once a week. Why don't sloths poop in trees? (The setup to another classic joke!) Some scientists think they do it that way to avoid making a lot of noise that could alert predators to their whereabouts. And think about it: sloths are so slow—reaching a max speed of about 0.9 miles (1.4 km) per hour and sleeping up to 20 hours a day—because it helps them stay hidden from predators, so why would they want to give away their location? The large predators that live with sloths in Central and South America, such as jaguars and eagles, can't spot the quiet, motionless, slightly greenish creatures. (Algae, not to mention moths and beetles, often grow in sloths' fur.)

ANSWER: WE DON'T KNOW, BUT IT MUST HAVE HAD A REALLY GOOD REASON!

WHAAAT?!

Sloths are slow and sleepy, but when they're attacked, they fight back with huge, strong claws.

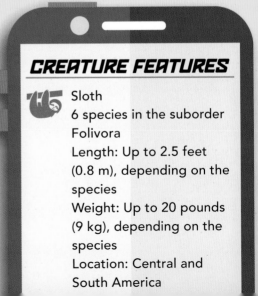

CREATURE FEATURES

Sloth
6 species in the suborder Folivora
Length: Up to 2.5 feet (0.8 m), depending on the species
Weight: Up to 20 pounds (9 kg), depending on the species
Location: Central and South America

WHAT WOULD HAPPEN IF A SNOWSHOE HARE WORE ACTUAL SNOWSHOES?

WHAT DO WE KNOW?

Well, why do snowshoe hares even have those big, furry snowshoe-like hind feet in the first place? For walking on snow. Just like the snowshoes you might strap on to walk on snow without sinking, a snowshoe hare's feet are wide to help spread out its weight. The hare has two predator-avoiding strategies: it can flee (leaping and zigzagging and reaching speeds of 35 miles—56 km—an hour) or it can freeze, hoping its camouflage coloring lets it go unseen. In the summer, snowshoe hares are brown-gray, and in the winter, they're white, except for the tips of their ears.

ANSWER: IF A SNOWSHOE HARE WORE ACTUAL SNOWSHOES, ASIDE FROM LOOKING SILLY, IT WOULD PROBABLY MAKE THE HARE'S LIFE DIFFICULT.

It would certainly interfere with its ability to walk and to remain hidden when predators are around. But big, giant snowshoes would make them stick out like snowshoe-wearing thumbs. They also thump their hind feet to send signals to each other. That's one thing real snowshoes might help with.

CREATURE FEATURES

Snowshoe hare
Lepus americanus
Length: Up to 20 inches (51 cm)
Weight: Up to 4 pounds (1.8 kg)
Location: The northern half of North America

WHAAAT?!

With their big, wide feet, snowshoe hares are good swimmers. Try doing *that* with snowshoes on.

DID TAPIRS INVENT SNORKELING?

WHAT DO WE KNOW?

Tapirs are considered primitive animals, because their basic shape hasn't changed much in tens of millions of years. They're also known for their trunks. A tapir's trunk is thinner and shorter than an elephant's trunk, and it has two tubular nostrils that almost seem to point in different directions. They use their trunks for picking up smells, for breathing, and for stripping leaves from branches, plucking fruit, and moving food to their mouths. They like spending time in the water to get cool, graze on water vegetation, and bathe. They can hold their breath for several minutes.

ANSWER: IN A WAY, YES.

Tapirs can use their stubby trunks to breathe when they're underwater. They can't breathe when they're completely submerged, though, so the trunk is more like a snorkel. And their bodies haven't changed in millions of years!

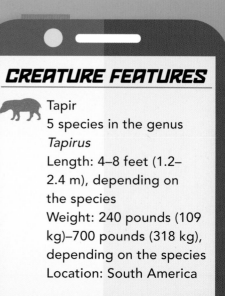

CREATURE FEATURES

Tapir
5 species in the genus *Tapirus*
Length: 4–8 feet (1.2–2.4 m), depending on the species
Weight: 240 pounds (109 kg)–700 pounds (318 kg), depending on the species
Location: South America

CAN A TASMANIAN DEVIL REALLY SPIN THROUGH YOUR WALL LIKE A TORNADO?

WHAT DO WE KNOW?

The Tasmanian devil is a small scavenger (and occasional predator) with an outsize power and toughness. Devils fill the night with their spine-chilling barks, hisses, and shrieks. And when they sink their teeth into a meal, they do it with the world's most powerful bite force for its size. That means that pound for pound, the devil has the strongest bite in the animal kingdom. Their jaws can crack bones, and devils eat everything, bones and hair included. They're so mean they yawn in the face of threats. Well, to be fair, it only looks like they're yawning. When they open their mouths wide and show off that impressive collection of teeth, they're actually expressing fear and stress. Bonus: they also produce a "special" (stinky) smell when they're stressed. In conclusion, you really don't want to bother Tasmanian devils.

CREATURE FEATURES

Tasmanian devil
Sarcophilus harrisii
Length: Up to 2.5 feet (0.8 m)
Weight: Up to 26 pounds (11.8 kg)
Location: Tasmania

ANSWER: NO, OF COURSE NOT.

But everybody's favorite cartoon Tasmanian devil isn't as much of an exaggeration as you might have thought, right.

COULD TIGERS SURVIVE IN THE DESERT?

WHAT DO WE KNOW?

Tigers are, of course, known for their orange-and-black-striped coat. They are stalk-and-pounce hunters that rely on camouflage and surprise to take down big mammals. But tigers often come up empty when they're hunting. Less than 10 percent of all tiger hunting attempts are successful.

ANSWER: NO. TIGERS ARE TOUGH AND STRONG, BUT THEY WOULD STILL HAVE A VERY HARD TIME IN THE DESERT.

Tigers are built for the jungle, and everything that makes them perfect for jungle life would be a big problem in the desert. Start with a tiger's coat. To a tiger's prey, the tiger's orange-and-black coat blends in with the tall grasses of their jungle environment. And the desert is no place to find the deer, wild pigs, and other prey that tigers like best. Just imagine if they had to make do with a bunch of little desert lizards. They'd never be able to fill up! And another thing: tigers like to cool off and swim in the water. And how could they do that if they lived in the desert?

WHAAAT?!

Tigers have been known to eat as much as 60 pounds (27 kg) in one sitting.

CREATURE FEATURES

Bengal tiger
Panthera tigris tigris
Length: Up to 9 feet (2.7 m), including the tail
Weight: Up to 500 pounds (227 kg)
Location: India, Southeast Asia, and East Asia

ARE VAMPIRE BATS THE DEADLIEST CREATURES OF THE NIGHT?

WHAT DO WE KNOW?

These little creatures land near a cow, a pig, a horse—and sometimes even a human. Unlike other bats, vampire bats are good at walking and running, and they use these skills to sneak closer to their prey. They use a special heat sensor on their noses to locate the best spot to bite (a spot where the blood vessels are just beneath the skin). They make a little cut with their very sharp teeth. And then they start lapping the blood that flows from the cut. A vampire bat's saliva contains substances called anticoagulants. These keep the blood from clotting, so it keeps the blood trickling out.

ANSWER: NOPE, NOT AT ALL.

Yes, they do emerge at night, and, yes, they do drink blood. But while they are definitely vampire-ish, they are not deadly. (Lots of nocturnal animals—bobcats and coyotes to name just a couple—are potentially way more dangerous.) Vampire bats are so gentle that their prey doesn't even wake up. The bat can keep feeding for up to 30 minutes, all without being detected.

CREATURE FEATURES

Common vampire bat
Desmodus rotundus
Wingspan: Up to 7 inches (18 cm)
Weight: Up to 2 ounces (57 g)
Location: Mexico and Central and South America

WHAAAT?!

Vampire bats have especially long thumbs. They use their thumbs to help them push off and jump up to take off after an especially big meal. (Yuck.)

WHAT WOULD HAPPEN IF A *WALRUS* WORE HANDCUFFS?

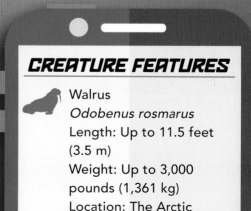

WHAT DO WE KNOW?

Each walrus—male and female alike—grows a pair of hefty, curving teeth that can be up to 3 feet (0.9 m) long! These amazing tusks keep growing throughout the walrus's life, and they are extremely useful. It sounds hard to believe, but a walrus uses its tusks like ice axes to help it haul its enormous bulk out of the water and onto the ice. (This is what led to the walrus's scientific name, which means "tooth-walking horse of the sea.") Walruses also stab the underside of the ice with their tusks to create breathing holes. Not only that, but the tusks come into play during extended walrus wrestling matches, when walruses battle it out for dominance and a little extra elbow room.

ANSWER: WE'RE GOING TO IGNORE THE FACT THAT THERE'S NO WAY A WALRUS COULD WEAR ACTUAL HANDCUFFS. BUT EVEN WITHOUT BEING ABLE TO USE THEIR HANDS (FLIPPERS), WALRUSES WOULD PROBABLY STILL DO ALL RIGHT.

CREATURE FEATURES

Walrus
Odobenus rosmarus
Length: Up to 11.5 feet (3.5 m)
Weight: Up to 3,000 pounds (1,361 kg)
Location: The Arctic

DO WILDEBEESTS LIKE TO PARTY?

WHAT DO WE KNOW?

These giant antelopes gather in huge numbers in Kenya's Maasai Mara National Reserve and wait until the time is right to begin their annual migration. It's all about following the rains and the good grazing they bring. The wildebeests set off with zebras and gazelles and make their way south, through the Serengeti National Park and other regions of Tanzania, dodging predators like lions, cheetahs, and hyenas as they go. Calves are born—as many as half a million of them!—and the gang keeps going. Next they'll need to slip past crocodiles waiting for them in the swollen rivers. A few months later, the survivors are back in the Maasai Mara, and they're preparing to start the whole circuit again.

ANSWER: YES—IF BY *PARTY*, WE MEAN "TRAVEL A THOUSAND MILES EVERY YEAR WITH MORE THAN A MILLION OF YOUR FRIENDS AND FAMILY MEMBERS, ALL WHILE AVOIDING PREDATORS AND DEALING WITH THE ELEMENTS." IN THAT CASE, WILDEBEESTS LOVE TO PARTY.

CREATURE FEATURES

Blue wildebeest
Connochaetes taurinus
Height: Up to 5 feet (1.5 m) at the shoulder
Weight: Up to 550 pounds (249 kg)
Location: Southern Africa

WHAAAT?!

A wildebeest calf can keep up with its mother when it's only 2 days old.

IS A WOLF GOOD AT KARAOKE?

WHAT DO WE KNOW?

Wolves, the biggest canine animals, are big singers. Or, you know, howlers. They sing for many reasons: to tell anyone within earshot that this is their territory, to call out to other members of the pack, to signal that game is nearby, and (hey, it's possible) even just to have fun. And like dogs, wolves howl when they hear others howling. This must be the equivalent of a catchy song spreading through the community. It's like a whole society that communicates by howling. Each pack even has its own special howl. It's not surprising that a wolf pack would want to bond. Wolves depend on their packs—usually around eight related wolves—for security and for hunting help. Wolf packs work together to bring down large prey animals, like deer, moose, and elk. When the pack is successful, the members sit down to eat together. And they can eat a lot. A wolf can pack away as much as 20 pounds (9 kg) in a single sitting.

ANSWER: YES. SINCE THEY HOWL FOR FUN, AND HOWL IN GROUPS, WE THINK THEY'D DO PRETTY WELL, PROBABLY.

CREATURE FEATURES

Gray wolf
Canis lupus
Length: Up to 7 feet (2.1 m), including the tail
Weight: Up to 175 pounds (79.4 kg)
Location: Canada, the northern United States, and Asia

WHAAAT?!

Scientists have taught a computer to listen to wolf howls and identify the individual wolf doing the howling.

DO WOLVERINES CONTROL AVALANCHES?

WHAT DO WE KNOW?

Wolverines don't let anything get between them and dinner. They have been known to try to steal kills from bears. And when they eat, they eat *well*. The wolverine's scientific name means "glutton," after all. They even eat teeth and bones! They hunt as well as they scavenge, and they take down everything from chipmunks to deer. They have big, wide paws with big, curved claws for walking on top of the snow.

ANSWER: NO. WHILE THEY DON'T CONTROL AVALANCHES, THEY DEFINITELY TAKE ADVANTAGE OF THEM.

Up in the snowy north, where wolverines live, avalanches are a frequent danger. And when a big wall of snow rolls down a mountain and buries everything in its path, wolverines are there with their supersensitive noses. They can sniff out the carcasses of avalanche (and big predator) victims, even deep under the snow.

WHAAAT?!

A wolverine's coat is thick and oily for great insulation in supercold temperatures.

CREATURE FEATURES

Wolverine
Gulo gulo
Length: Up to 4 feet (1.2 m), including the tail
Weight: Up to 40 pounds (18 kg)
Location: Around the world, in the subarctic

WHAT'S SO GREAT ABOUT A WOMBAT BUTT?

WHAT DO WE KNOW?

Wombats have two main predators: dingoes and Tasmanian devils (read about Tasmanian devils on page 119 of this book), and those things are tough customers. If they chase a wombat, it runs and leaps into its burrow, presenting its strong backside. The predator can't get past the hairy roadblock. And a wombat's butt has a tiny tail and very thick skin, so it can stand up to powerful bites.

ANSWER: A WOMBAT'S BUTT IS A SHIELD. AND IT'S ALSO A WEAPON.

A wombat can use it to push a predator's head against the ceilings and walls of its burrow.

CREATURE FEATURES

Wombat
3 species in the family
Vombatidae
Length: Up to 2.5 feet
(0.8 m)
Weight: 40 pounds
(18 kg)–90 pounds (41 kg),
depending on the species
Location: Southern
Australia

WHAAAT?!

Wombats are tremendous diggers. The tunnels of wombat burrows can stretch more than 600 feet (183 m).

WHAT'S WITH THE ZEBRA DRESS CODE?

WHAT DO WE KNOW?

A prey animal better have a really good reason for sticking out as much as zebras do. They don't blend in at all! How can you hide from predators like lions and spotted hyenas if you're wearing such eye-catching outfits? One theory says that the stripes are confusing to predators, who might not be able to zero in on a particular animal in a herd of running zebras. The stripes would make the zebras look like they were all jumbled together. Recent studies suggest this might not be true. So how come zebras wear stripes? Computer models show that zebras in hotter areas have more stripes. Air passing over a black-and-white surface seems to cool down. (The skin of zebras with lots of stripes is more than several degrees cooler than the skin of animals with no stripes.) And annoying and disease-carrying pests such as horseflies like hotter conditions and don't like to land on stripes!

ANSWER: PUT IT ALL TOGETHER, AND IT LOOKS LIKE ZEBRA STRIPES ARE ALL ABOUT STAYING COOL AND BUG-FREE.

CREATURE FEATURES

Plains zebra
Equus quagga
Length: Up to 5 feet (1.5 m) at the shoulder
Weight: Up to 990 pounds (449 kg)
Location: Southern Africa

REPTILES

To understand reptiles, you need to look on the outside and the inside. Outside-wise, reptiles are covered in scales or bony plates, or both. Inside-wise, reptiles are cold-blooded. This means that, unlike mammals, for instance, reptiles' bodies can't regulate or adjust their temperature from the inside. If they want to warm up, reptiles need to find a sunny spot (or make sure to live in a hot place). If they want to cool down, they need to find shade or head into the water. Being cold-blooded also usually means having a slow metabolism and a generally slow lifestyle. Some reptiles can go months or even more than a year between meals!

COULD YOU JUMP ROPE WITH AN ANACONDA?

WHAT DO WE KNOW?

Anacondas are huge. At up to 30 feet (9.1 m) long and 550 pounds (249 kg), they're the biggest snakes in the world. To get so big, they eat big prey, like wild pigs, deer, and capybaras, and even bigger animals, like jaguars. Their eyes and nostrils are high up on their heads, so they can stay mostly submerged in the water as they wait patiently for prey. And the way they go after it is a little upsetting: they pounce, loop coils around their prey, and squeeze and squeeze and squeeze. (Sometimes they also pull their prey underwater and drown it.) And then comes the truly unpleasant part: the opening-wide-and-swallowing-the-prey-whole part. After that, they can go for months without a meal.

ANSWER: NO, NO, AND NO. NOT EVEN IF YOU COULD FIND A BUNCH OF KIDS WILLING TO TRY THIS WITH YOU.

Anacondas are way too big and heavy to be jump ropes. Besides being too bulky, anacondas are too dangerous—and they eat child-size prey. So do yourself a favor: keep your hands off the anaconda.

CREATURE FEATURES

Green anaconda
Eunectes murinus
Length: Up to 30 feet (9.1 m)
Weight: Up to 550 pounds (249 kg)
Location: South America

WHAT HAPPENS IF A CHAMELEON GETS MAD?

WHAT DO WE KNOW?

Chameleons have grasping tails, clasping hands, independently roving eyes, and superfast sticky tongues. But their most famous characteristic is their ability to change colors.

ANSWER: THEY SEE RED! OR, ACTUALLY, YOU'LL SEE RED, YELLOW, OR ORANGE. THEY SHOW THEIR EMOTIONS BY CHANGING COLORS.

Chameleons change hues for lots of reasons. It can help them blend into their surroundings, keep cool in Africa's heat, and communicate with each other.

But scientists also think that chameleons color-change like mood rings: Their shade shows how they feel. A happy, calm chameleon is green or brown to match their surroundings, which are usually trees or the forest floor. But get a chameleon mad—like when it's aggressively defending its territory from another chameleon—and it will turn an angry red, yellow, or orange.

Chameleons' color also communicates when they're feeling down or when they've lost a fight: their coloring dulls or turns darker.

Location: East Africa and Madagascar, but also the Middle East, India, Spain, and Portugal

CREATURE FEATURES

Chameleon
Family Chamaeleonidae
Length: Up to 27 inches
(68.6 cm) in the
largest species
Weight: 1.5 pounds
(0.68 kg)

WHAT IF YOU GIVE A GECKO A HAIRCUT?

WHAT DO WE KNOW?

Now, just a second! Geckos are reptiles, and reptiles don't have hair! (Only mammals have hair. It's one of the things that makes a mammal a mammal.)

But, on the bottom of a gecko's feet, on the bottom of its toe pads, are millions and millions of teeny, tiny hairlike things called setae (SEE-tee). When these setae come in contact with a smooth surface, something geck-tacular—ahem, spectacular—happens: a strong bond is formed, and the gecko sticks to the surface. It's not suction cups. It's not gooey stuff. It's just many, many little forces that draw the setae to the surface. Add up all those forces, and it's enough to keep the gecko stuck so it doesn't fall.

ANSWER: IF YOU GAVE A GECKO A "HAIRCUT"—OR SETAE CUT—IT COULDN'T DO WHAT IT DOES.

WHAAAT?!

Two bonus gecko facts: 1) their tails can detach and flip around all over the place to distract a predator, and 2) geckos clean their eyes with their tongues.

CREATURE FEATURES

Gecko
About 1,777 species in the suborder Gekkota
Length: Less than 1 inch (2.5 cm)–1.5 feet (0.5 m)
Weight: Less than 1 ounce (28 g: they are tiny)–less than 0.6 pounds (272 g)
Location: Worldwide, but mostly in the Southern Hemisphere

WOULD A KING COBRA MAKE A GOOD KING?

WHAT DO WE KNOW?

King cobras are interesting snakes. They growl, for one thing, and they can climb trees. As if a growling, climbing snake wasn't scary enough, king cobras can be aggressive. They rear up, raising their heads high off the ground and pursuing prey like that. A king cobra could look you in the eye and follow you around. But it probably wouldn't because king cobras would rather eat other snakes, even venomous ones! They sink their sharply angled teeth into their prey and deliver a big dose of deadly neurotoxin that stops a prey animal's breathing.

ANSWER: NO. KINGS IN STORYBOOKS ARE KIND AND BENEVOLENT. KING COBRAS ARE AGGRESSIVE AND SCARY.

If a king cobra was a king, it would be a terrifying king leading an army to war. Instead of a flag, it would have that big, flattened hood it spreads out around its head when it gets all worked up.

CREATURE FEATURES

King cobra
Ophiophagus hannah
Length: Up to 18 feet (5.5 m)
Weight: Up to 20 pounds (9 kg)
Location: India, China, Indonesia, and the Philippines

WHAAAT?!

A single king cobra bite can inject enough venom to kill an elephant.

WHAT'S GREEN, SHARP, AND TOUGH? IGUANA TELL YOU!

WHAT DO WE KNOW?

Congratulations! You just found the worst joke in this book.

ANSWER: BUT REALLY, IGUANAS ARE PRETTY COOL.

Just by looking at them, you can see some of what makes them special: their size, their coloring, the crest of spines down their backs, and their sharp teeth and tails. They even have a "third eye" (a light-receptive spot on the tops of their heads)!

But like with humans, it's what's inside that counts. And on the inside, iguanas are tough. They are fast, and they can withstand falls of 40 feet (12 m). (They like to hang out in trees and will jump to escape from predators.) Being lizards, iguanas are cold-blooded. That means they depend on their environment for warmth. So they love lounging around in the sun. (They're plant-eaters, so they don't have the kind of rush-rush lifestyle that hunters often lead.) During exceptionally cold winters, iguanas get so cold they stop moving, and sometimes they even fall out of trees with a thump. It's a good thing they're so tough.

CREATURE FEATURES

Green iguana
Iguana iguana
Length: Up to 6.5 feet (2 m)
Weight: Up to 11 pounds (5 kg)
Location: Mexico, Central America, and northern South America

WHAAAT?!

Q: When are green iguanas not green?

A: Lots of times! Green iguanas can be brown, gray, and black. And the males are orange during mating season!

WHAT'S IT LIKE TO BE KISSED BY A KOMODO DRAGON?

WHAT DO WE KNOW?

Komodo dragons often have strings of drool hanging out of their mouths. That's gross just because, but it's even grosser because their saliva is filled with deadly bacteria. As bad as a Komodo dragon's bite is, it's the bacteria that really do a number on the Komodo dragon's prey. Yes, the dragons have very sharp teeth—and they even make venom in their mouths. There's also bacteria. Those sharp teeth have little ridges, like a steak knife's serrated edge. Bits of meat collect in those little ridges, and lots of bacteria form, leading to bites filled with nasty stuff. Not much escapes a Komodo dragon attack—these are big, powerful hunters, after all—but a prey animal that gets away with only a bite or two will soon succumb to the deadly bacteria now in its wound. And the Komodo dragon venom keeps the animal's wound from healing. It's a lethal one-two punch.

ANSWER: JUST AWFUL— EVEN DEADLY!

Do not under any circumstances allow a Komodo dragon to kiss you. They are the world's worst kissers.

WHAAAT?!

A Komodo dragon can smell carrion (dead animals) from more than 2 miles (3.2 km) away. A Komodo dragon can eat 80 percent of its body weight in one meal.

KISS_ BOOTH

NLY $1!

CREATURE FEATURES

Komodo dragon
Varanus komodoensis
Length: Up to 10.5 feet
(3.2 m)
Weight: Up to 366 pounds
(166 kg)
Location: Small islands in
Indonesia

DO NILE CROCODILES MAKE GOOD BABYSITTERS?

WHAT DO WE KNOW?

Until the babies are 2 years old or so, Nile crocodiles are excellent caretakers. It starts when the mother croc lays the eggs—as many as 60 of them—and then watches over them for months. (The father croc is often nearby, ready to pitch in.) The babies signal that they're ready to hatch by making a series of squeaks. Mom helps any croclings having trouble emerging from their eggs by gently rolling the eggs in her mouth. Then she scoops the babies up in her jaws, carries them in her throat sac, and brings them to the water for their first swim. Until they're ready to move out on their own, the youngsters will eat fish and bugs at Mom's side.

ANSWER: OF SOMEONE ELSE'S KIDS? THAT'S NOT RECOMMENDED. OF THEIR OWN KIDS? DEFINITELY!

When it comes to taking care of their own babies, Nile crocodiles are much more tender than you might expect.

CREATURE FEATURES

Nile crocodile
Crocodylus niloticus
Length: Up to 20 feet (6 m)
Weight: Up to 1,650 pounds (748 kg)
Location: Much of Africa

DO RATTLESNAKES LIKE THEIR RATTLES?

WHAT DO WE KNOW?

A rattlesnake uses its rattle to warn possible predators (even rattlesnakes have predators) that it's there. A predator might decide to clear out instead of dealing with a rattler. Rattlesnakes add another segment to their rattlers every year.

But like all snakes, rattlers have no ears. They hear by sensing vibrations that move through the ground. And seeing as they have no legs, and they're always pressed against the ground, they can pick up a lot of sensory information that way. They hear without ears, so maybe it's not surprising that they smell with their tongues. When a rattler flicks its forked tongue in and out, what it's doing is picking up particles in the air and bringing them to a special organ in the roof of its mouth to smell them.

ANSWER: IF THIS MEANS "DO RATTLESNAKES TREASURE THEIR USEFUL RATTLES?" THEN THE ANSWER IS PROBABLY YES.

But if the question means "Do rattlesnakes enjoy the sound their rattles make?" then the answer is probably no.

CREATURE FEATURES

Rattlesnake
About 30 species in the genera *Crotalus* and *Sistrurus*
Length: 1 foot (30 cm)–8 feet (2.4 m), depending on the species
Weight: 4 ounces (113 g)–10 pounds (4.5 kg), depending on the species
Location: Much of the United States, Mexico, and Central and South America

141

HOW ARE SEA TURTLES LIKE LOTTERY WINNERS?

WHAT DO WE KNOW?

Sea turtles don't have it easy. They travel huge distances from their feeding grounds to their nesting grounds. A sea turtle will make a nest in the sand on the same beach where it hatched. (A sea turtle could be 30 years old before laying its first batch of eggs, but it knows where to go.) The female lays as many as 200 eggs, covers them up, and returns to the ocean. A couple of months later, the eggs hatch, and the new sea turtles face the most dangerous time of their lives: the short journey from the nest to the water. Crabs and seagulls are waiting for them. The sea turtles that make it through the gauntlet of predators on the beach must survive the predators in the water.

ANSWER: BECAUSE THEY REALLY BATTLE THE ODDS. SOME SCIENTISTS THINK THAT ONLY ABOUT 1 IN 10,000 HATCHLINGS MAKES IT ALL THE WAY TO ADULTHOOD.

WHAAAT?!

Baby sea turtles hatch with the help of a special "egg tooth," a pointy nub on its face.

CREATURE FEATURES

Green sea turtle
Chelonia mydas
Length: Up to 3 feet (0.9 m)
Weight: Up to 350 pounds (159 kg)
Location: Much of the Atlantic and Pacific Oceans

TORTOISES CAN BE OLD, BUT CAN THEY BE WISE?

WHAT DO WE KNOW?

Tortoises are among the longest-living animals on the planet. Giant tortoises, which live in the Galápagos Islands off the coast of Ecuador, can live to be more than 150 years old. There are reports of a giant tortoise that made it past his 180th birthday.

ANSWER: NO. NOT IN THE SENSE OF SITTING ON A PORCH SWING WITH YOU AND GIVING YOU GRANDFATHERLY LIFE ADVICE. BUT TORTOISES ARE SMARTER THAN MANY PEOPLE THOUGHT POSSIBLE.

When researchers put red-footed tortoises to the test, they discovered that the slow-moving beasts were able to do some surprising things. They could learn to complete tricky tasks by watching other red-footed tortoises do them. That might not sound like much, but before this, scientists believed only social animals could learn by watching others of their kind. And tortoises aren't even close to social. They don't form groups, and they don't give their babies any care at all.

CREATURE FEATURES

Tortoise
About 50 species in the family Testudinidae
Length: 4.5 inches (11.4 cm)–4.5 feet (1.4 m)
Weight: Less than 1 pound (454 g)–920 pounds (417 kg)
Location: Worldwide

WHAAAT?!

Other surprising things tortoises can do: follow other tortoises' gaze (look where they're looking) and make mental maps. For reptiles, this is big stuff.

Brimming with creative inspiration, how-to projects, and useful information to enrich your everyday life, Quarto Knows is a favorite destination for those pursuing their interests and passions. Visit our site and dig deeper with our books into your area of interest: Quarto Creates, Quarto Cooks, Quarto Homes, Quarto Lives, Quarto Drives, Quarto Explores, Quarto Gifts, or Quarto Kids.

© 2020 Quarto Publishing Group USA Inc.

Published in 2020 by becker&mayer! kids, an imprint of The Quarto Group, 11120 NE 33rd Place, Suite 201, Bellevue, WA 98004 USA. **www.QuartoKnows.com**

becker&mayer! kids titles are also available at discount for retail, wholesale, promotional, and bulk purchase. For details, contact the Special Sales Manager by email at specialsales@quarto.com or by mail at The Quarto Group, Attn: Special Sales Manager, 100 Cummings Center Suite 265D, Beverly, MA 01915 USA.

21 22 23 24 25   7 6 5 4 3

ISBN: 978-0-7603-6888-6

Library of Congress Cataloging-in-Publication Data available upon request.

Printed, manufactured, and assembled in China, 04/21

MIX
Paper from responsible sources
FSC® C016973

Image credits: Mogens Trolle/Shutterstock.com, Keneva Photography/Shutterstock.com, Elsa Hoffmann/Shutterstock.com, wildestanimal/Shutterstock.com, Kambiz Pourghanad/Shutterstock.com, Inger Eriksen/Shutterstock.com, MyImages – Micha/Shutterstock.com, Yasser El Dershaby/Shutterstock.com, Andrew Sutton/Shutterstock.com, JonathanC Photography/Shutterstock.com, Nick Couckuyt/Shutterstock.com, Abeselom Zerit/Shutterstock.com, Warren Metcalf/Shutterstock.com, Dmytro Gilitukha/Shutterstock.com, Andrea Izzotti/Shutterstock.com, Lee Yiu Tung/Shutterstock.com, BYUNGSUK KO/Shutterstock.com, NikkiHoff/Shutterstock.com, Spartak Dolov/Shutterstock.com, David Rasmus/Shutterstock.com, Coatesy/Shutterstock.com, Tatiana Grozetskaya/Shutterstock.com, francesco de marco/Shutterstock.com, Maksim Shmeljov/Shutterstock.com, F_N/Shutterstock.com, Ollyy/Shutterstock.com, Albie Venter/Shutterstock.com, Jim Lambert/Shutterstock.com, apple2499/Shutterstock.com, Hedrus/Shutterstock.com, Alta Oosthuizen/Shutterstock.com, nattanan726/Shutterstock.com, Yusnizam Yusof/Shutterstock.com, tjp55/Shutterstock.com, Gunter Ziesler/Getty Images, gillmar/Shutterstock.com, Gecko1968/Shutterstock.com, Sonsedska Yuliia/Shutterstock.com, Chelsea Cameron/Shutterstock.com, WOLF AVNI/Shutterstock.com, Menno Schaefer/Shutterstock.com, Debbie Steinhausser/Shutterstock.com, FotoRequest/Shutterstock.com, Parkol/Shutterstock.com, Sander Groffen/Shutterstock.com, belizar/Shutterstock.com, Vaclav Volrab/Shutterstock.com, Aleksei Verhovski/Shutterstock.com, AndreAnita/Shutterstock.com, photos martYmage/Shutterstock.com, Paul Looyen/Shutterstock.com, prapass/Shutterstock.com, Holger Kirk/Shutterstock.com, CappaPhoto/Shutterstock.com, nico99/Shutterstock.com, Susan Schmitz/Shutterstock.com, Rostislav Stach/Shutterstock.com, Gaschwald/Shutterstock.com, Embrace of Beauty/Shutterstock.com, Julian W/Shutterstock.com, FOTOGRIN/Shutterstock.com, Willyam Bradberry/Shutterstock.com, michelaubryphoto/Shutterstock.com, Eric Isselee/Shutterstock.com, bluehand/Shutterstock.com, Andreas Meyer/Shutterstock.com, Onyx9/Shutterstock.com, Dirk Ercken/Shutterstock.com, Seokhee Kim/Shutterstock.com, feathercollector/Shutterstock.com, Dn Br/Shutterstock.com, lynea/Shutterstock.com, Artur Balytskyi/Shutterstock.com, vladsilver/Shutterstock.com, Jan Martin Will/Shutterstock.com, Andreas Meyer/Shutterstock.com, Leksele/Shutterstock.com, Eric Isselee/Shutterstock.com, Ondrej Prosicky/Shutterstock.com, Nicky Rhodes/Shutterstock.com, YK/Shutterstock.com, Andy Deitsch/Shutterstock.com, Kletr/Shutterstock.com, magnusdeepbelow/Shutterstock.com, J. Henning Buchholz/Shutterstock.com, Rich Carey/Shutterstock.com, Ariel Bravy/Shutterstock.com, Artur_Sarkisyan/Shutterstock.com, Aries Sutanto/Shutterstock.com, Protasov AN/Shutterstock.com, Bennyartist/Shutterstock.com, johannviloria/Shutterstock.com, KASIRA SUDA/Shutterstock.com, Ian_Sherriffs/Shutterstock.com, Sean Xu/Shutterstock.com, Danita Delmont/Shutterstock.com, Laurel A Egan/Shutterstock.com, GOLFX/Shutterstock.com, Vojce/Shutterstock.com, Stanislav Fosenbauer/Shutterstock.com, pickypalla/Shutterstock.com, Rudmer Zwerver/Shutterstock.com, 3445128471/Shutterstock.com, Robert Eastman/Shutterstock.com, FRDMR/Shutterstock.com, Aaron Amat/Shutterstock.com, Mike Price/Shutterstock.com, Tory Kallman/Shutterstock.com, 2630ben/Shutterstock.com, seeshooteatrepeat/Shutterstock.com, Eric Isselee/Shutterstock.com, Stephen Frink/Getty Images, Barbara Strnadova/Getty Images, GraphicsRF/Shutterstock.com, cellistka/Shutterstock.com, Audrey Snider-Bell/Shutterstock.com, Brian E Kushner/Shutterstock.com, Neil Bromhall/Shutterstock.com, Wiratchai wansamngam/Shutterstock.com, VisionDive/Shutterstock.com, Bildagentur Zoonar GmbH/Shutterstock.com, summer/Shutterstock.com, psv/Shutterstock.com, NattapolStudiO/Shutterstock.com, Jane Rix/Shutterstock.com, Krzysztof Odziomek/Shutterstock.com, De Agostini Picture Library/De Agostini/Getty Images, Martin Good/Shutterstock.com

#338479